Wood Carving

FREDA SKINNER

Wood Carving

Illustrated by Constance Morton

BONANZA BOOKS
New York

Acknowledgments

The author is indebted to the following for help and advice:
Gene Yerganian, for adaptation of this book for America;
J. Johnson & Co., of Manhasset, Long Island, New York, manufacturer and preparer of woods for carving and cutting, for information on woods available in America;
The Timber Development Association, 21, College Hill, London, E.C.4., for the diagrams on the structure of wood;
The Forests Research Laboratory, Princes Risborough, Bucks;
William Mallison and Sons, Ltd., 130, Hackney Road, London, E.2., suppliers of seasoned wood for 'The Risen Christ in Glory';
The Editor of 'Wood', 33, Tothill Street, London, S.W.1.;
Croid Ltd., Berkshire House, 168–173, High Holborn, London, W.C.1., glue specialists;
C.I.B.A. A.R.L. Ltd., of Duxford, Cambridge, England, glue specialists;
The Royal Veterinary College, Royal College Street, London, N.W.1.;
Harold Board, Architectural Carver, Merivale Road, London, S.W.15.;
Mr William Fagg, Deputy Keeper, Department of Ethnography, British Museum.

Contents

Introduction

A famous painter, when asked, 'How do I learn to paint?'
answered: 'Take a canvas, take a brush, dip the brush in the
paint and start.' Similar advice can be given in all seriousness to
the aspiring carver, for the best teachers in the world are practice
and, of course, the strong urge to fashion something for its own
sake.

In wood you have chosen one of the most beautiful, but also
one of the most exacting media. If you are carving a design in
which you are interested, if your tools are sharp, and the wood
is moving smoothly away from the sharp edge of the tool like
silk, wood carving is sheer pleasure. If, on the other hand, you
are uncertain of your design, the tool is blunt, the wood splitting
and ragging, and you are faced with a shapeless lump of timber,
wood carving is then, without doubt, sheer misery. My main
objective, therefore, in writing this book is to help you to design,
and advisedly I put design first, and then to carve your designs
in such a way that you create something really your own. It is
important that in these days of mass production we do not lose
sight of the inborn ability to use mind and hands together in
personal creation.

Wood always retains something of its living quality. It is
strong with the tensile strength of a fibrous material. It is infinitely
varied in the qualities of density, weight and durability. Although
vulnerable under certain conditions to fungi and insect attack,
we know on evidence that wood has been carved for three
thousand years and a few Egyptian wood carvings dating
about 2600 B.C. are still extant. There is something about the
very names of woods like ebony, snakewood, lignum vitae,
that summons up thoughts of the dark forests and tropical

shades where our ancestors started to carve in bone, wood and stone.

The qualities and sap life of timber mean that some understanding is necessary in order to make the best use of this material. In the following chapters I have tried to give a guide to those who wish to carve in wood. The book does not cover carpentry and joinery. These skills can be of great value to the carver, and those who are also interested in construction would profit by lessons in general woodwork to be used in conjunction with carving.

CHAPTER ONE

Wood

The tree

The study of wood has become a science in itself. Students who wish to go deeply into this subject can obtain detailed information from the Agricultural Research Service and the Forest Service divisions of the Department of Agriculture, Washington, D.C. Some general information, however, seems appropriate here so that the reader may gain a working understanding of his material.

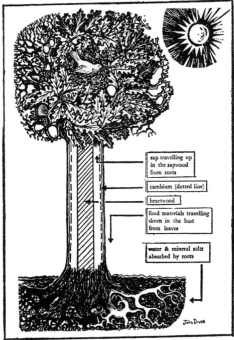

Fig. 1. The living tree (drawing by John Dives).

A tree can be said to have three component parts: the root, the trunk, and the crown. The roots absorb water and chemical substances from the soil which are carried by the sapwood to the leaves and branches of the tree. The bark of the tree is for protection and insulation. The growth and thickness of the trunk is

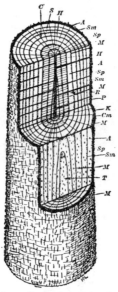

Fig. 2. Diagram of a log of wood, cut to show cross, radial, and tangential sections. C. Cross section. R. Radial section. T. Tangential section. S. Sapwood. H. Heartwood. A. Annual ring. Sm. Summerwood. Sp. Springwood. M. Medullary ray. P. Pith. K. Bark. Cm. cambium.

brought about by cambiumnial cells situated just under the bark of the tree. These cells eventually become sapwood which in turn becomes the heartwood as the tree grows in size and strength. In the so-called 'heartwood' trees, the difference in color of heartwood and sapwood can be clearly seen. A sawcut across a log of elm or yew will reveal the light, outer ring of sapwood and the dark, rich center of heartwood. The latter has now ceased to function as a carrier of sap and the cells are filled by resins and pigment. The function of this heartwood can be likened to a strong scaffold holding the tree erect. The sapwood is more vulnerable to attacks by fungi and insects whereas the heartwood is harder and more durable. The color difference between the two types

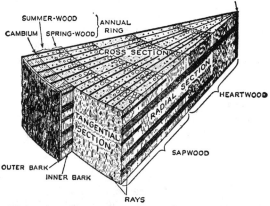

Fig. 3. Wedge-shaped segment cut from a five-year-old stem of hardwood, showing the principal structural features.

of wood is not always apparent; beech, lime, silver fir are cases in point.

In temperate countries annual rings of native woods, marking each year's growth, can be clearly seen, and usually by the naked eye. In early spring the growth starts rapidly and large spongy cells are formed. These constitute the soft spring-wood. As the summer progresses, the cells formed are smaller and harder, also they are slower in growth. It follows then that each annual ring has two parts, the broader spring-wood and narrower band of summer growth. When these annual rings can be clearly seen, as described, we speak of 'ring porous' woods. Examples of these

are ash, elm, and oak. During the autumn and winter the tree
rests and growth ceases. The rate of growth varies a great deal
according to species, climate and altitude. In tropical countries
trees such as ebony, continue to grow all the year round and there
are no marked rings, only areas of growth.

Broadly, we can divide trees into two groups: 'softwoods', or
those belonging to the conifae, like firs and pines, and 'hardwoods', belonging to the dicotyledonae, or broad leaved varieties.
As in the case of all generalizations, careful study discovers
subdivisions of this rule. The softwoods belong to a more
primitive and simple type of tree structure, while the hardwoods are far more complex in form. These are botanical
terms and do not refer to actual hardness or softness.

Seasoning and shrinkage

In air and kiln seasoning, time depends on the density, thickness and water content of the wood. It is not advisable to use
green, freshly cut timber for carving. The cells and the cell walls
of this timber contain water. It is the process of drying out the
free water in the cells, and the partial drying out of water in the
cell walls, which is known as 'seasoning'. It is obvious that when
this water—which is after all a part of the tree's composition—is
removed, shrinkage is bound to take place. Therefore the process
must be controlled if distortion, cracks and splits are to be
avoided. The two main methods of seasoning are air seasoning
and kiln drying. The former is a slow method. For instance, with
2-in. planks it will take over six months of good drying weather
to reduce the moisture content of twenty per cent of their weight.
For timber used in heated buildings it is necessary to reduce the
moisture to about ten to twelve per cent. The process of seasoning
wood in a modern kiln can be achieved in a matter of weeks. In
the case of tropical woods, air seasoning is favored, for periods
up to two years. These can then be finally dried by the kiln
method. There are a few woods that cannot be kilned at all
as the cell walls of the wood collapse and render the wood
useless.

The kiln

Very briefly, the kiln is a brick-built room with heating pipes generally in the ceiling. Fans are installed to keep the air moving and steam is introduced through a number of jets. The wood is stacked horizontally in such a way that the air can circulate freely. The planks themselves rest on 'sticks' or wood bearers of 1 in. × 1 in., spaced approximately 4 ft. apart for planks that are 2 in. thick or more. Regular tests of moisture content during kilning are made and the drying process is controlled by varying the humidity and the heat.

Air seasoning

Timber deteriorates if left on the ground and exposed to the elements. In air seasoning the timber is stacked, as in kiln drying, in such a way that the air can circulate. The stack should not be more than 6 ft. wide. A well-drained site is chosen and brick piers are built not less than 9 in. in height and preferably more. These piers are approximately 9 in. square and are spaced 2 ft. apart. Timber cross-members 4 in. × 4 in. are placed on the piers. Strength is given by laying further heavy bearers along the whole length of the stack. The planks to be seasoned are placed horizontally on the foundation, each plank separated from the other by 1 in. × 1 in. sticks. It is important that the wood should be kept level and sagging prevented. Therefore, the sticks are placed at intervals of 2 ft. to 4 ft., according to the thickness of the planks. The stack is left open but covered by a sloping roof with a good overhang. The ends of the planks should be protected by bituminous paint. In reasonable weather, 2-in. planks of softwood stacked in the spring would be seasoned by the autumn of the same year. Hardwoods should be stacked three months earlier.

Conversion of timber

Conversion is a term used to describe the cutting of wood into planks. In figure 4 you will see the 'through and through' cut or slash-sawn log. This is the most economical form of cutting timber but there is a greater tendency to warping, as shown in B. In C and D you will see two methods of quarter cutting. The center picture shows the more common form when the center is 'boxed out', that is cut away. Quarter cutting is used in oak in order to show the silver grain or medullary rays.

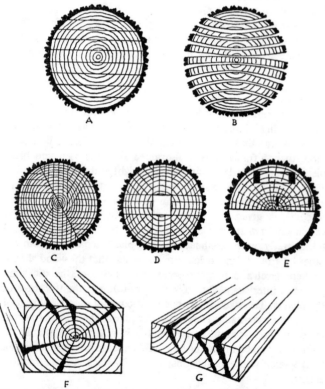

Fig. 4. Cutting and shrinkage. A. 'Through and through' cut. B. Shrinkage in a plain-sawn log. C. Quarter sawing, one method. D. Quarter sawing, the usual method. E. Relative shrinkage in slash-sawn and quarter-sawn boards; the shaded part indicates the amount of shrinkage. F. Star-shakes. G. End splits.

Shrinkage

The greatest amount of shrinkage takes place in the tangential direction of the log, which means along the line of the annual rings at a tangent to the circumference of the log. The radial shrinkage is only half as much. Figure 4, E shows in black shading the relative shrinkage of a slash-sawn and quarter-sawn board. Uneven drying causes uneven shrinkage and various splits and checks can develop. Two examples, star-shakes and end splits, are illustrated (Fig. 4, F and G).

Fungal decay and insect attack

In the ordinary way, fungal decay and insect attack are not likely to trouble the wood carver. However, you can, if you wish, treat your carving with a wood preservative when the work is completed.

Fungus, the chief cause of decay in timber, is a plant and needs organic material to maintain life. It must also have moisture and oxygen so that wood kept dry will not be attacked. Whereas it is highly unlikely that your carving will be attacked by fungi, insect pests can easily move from infected furniture to your work. The most common of these pests is the furniture beetle (*anobium punctatum*), often known as 'wood worm'. During June and until August the beetles emerge from the wood looking for new homes in any suitable cracks and crevices in timber. Both hard- and softwoods are vulnerable. The insects then lay their eggs. These eventually hatch into larvae a quarter of an inch long. With powerful jaws these grubs bore into the wood. This process goes on for as long as eighteen months when the grub pupates and the whole cycle commences again. It is possible to treat wood with chemicals toxic to both fungi and insects. There are a number of proprietary brands on the market.

Durability of wood

The durability of wood is not related to its hardness or softness. When the term is used in the timber trade, it refers to the wood's reaction to climate, weather conditions, contact with the ground, immersion in water, etc. Wood carvings are, as a rule, under roof protection and it will therefore be only on occasion that a carver must consider durability as a factor in his work.

Timbers grown in the United States, such as oak and elm, are durable woods. Some softwoods are extremely durable, as for instance red cedar, which is more durable than oak. Resins, tannin and aromatic oils in the wood form together an effective preservative.

CHAPTER TWO

Wood for carving

WOODS, like so many materials we use, are subject to fashion.
For instance, pitch pine and mahogany suffered an eclipse at the
close of the nineteenth century but now they are again gaining
favor. Fresh treatments and new designs make us see these
woods in a different light. Those who can look back far enough
remember the pitch pine school desks, still surviving in the
1920's. They were usually ink-stained and scarred and for
me associated with being 'kept in' on sunny afternoons. Now
less pitch pine is imported but the strong resin-filled grain with its
striking pattern would lend itself to modern treatment. A wood
craftsman I met recently talked sadly of the time when he burned
quantities of pitch pine veneer because at that time it was out of
fashion and unsalable. Of course, some woods are more pleasant
to carve than others. Some will carve in almost any direction,
others are stubborn with difficult grain, and some blunt the
tools.

In this chapter I describe some thirty-five woods which are
suitable for carving. The carver should be ready to try any variety
of wood that comes his way, provided it is seasoned and little
expense is involved. Woods new to this country are continually
being imported and exciting discoveries can be made. A few
minutes' work will show the carving qualities of a new wood. The
amateur, carving just for his own pleasure, can afford time to
experiment on small pieces while the professional carver tends to
use woods already proved. When you go to a lumber or timber
yard do not be put off by the look of the outside of a stack of
timber. Sometimes it is stacked in the open under a roof but not
closed in, a method also used in air seasoning. At first glance the
wood may look a uniform grey but its true color will not be
revealed until the wood is cut or carved. Wood as a material is
invariably of great interest to those who work with it and in a

timber yard you might possibly find men who have been in the trade for years. You will find them knowledgeable and very ready to tell you all they know. Wood that works easily in their machines is likely to carve well also.

In the following descriptions the weight in parentheses is the approximate weight per cubic foot of air-seasoned timber.

White Afara (30–40 lb.). A straw-colored wood, this is a general utility hardwood. It will carve reasonably well and is even in texture. Afara splits very readily and takes glue, stain and polish well. It is often used for turned work and parquet flooring. Afara is grown in tropical Africa.

Red Alder (28 lb.). Red alder is easy to work and finishes well. It is durable even in damp climates.

Crab Apple (46 lb.). The color is pinkish grey to light brown and the wood is suitable for fine carving. It is hard and heavy. Unfortunately the tree does not grow to more than 12 in. in diameter as a general rule. The wood takes a fine natural polish with handling. It is used for mallet heads, drawing instruments, saw handles and other purposes where a fine-grained, reliable timber is required.

Ash (45 lb.). Color white to light brown. Ash is a rather tough wood to carve but not excessively so. The grain is broad in character and strongly marked. Other uses: furniture, axe- and hammer-shafts, hoops and rims.

Basswood (26 lb.). Easily workable and soft enough that you may dispense with your mallet, this wood tends to brittleness and is susceptible to decay. Especially useful for woodenware, it takes stain well and can be finished to a fine luster.

Beech (45–50 lb.). Beech varies in color from greyish pink to warm light red. It is plentiful in America and used widely in the furniture trade. It is a reliable all-purpose hardwood, with an even texture that can be worked in all directions. It carves and polishes well and will readily take stain.

Boxwood (60 lb.). Boxwood is remarkable for its uniform yellow color. It is almost like ivory in that it will take very small carved detail without breaking. Boxwood was used extensively in the seventeenth century for small figure carving. Unfortunately, owing to the bush-like nature of the tree, the sizes are small. It is commonly used for chessmen, modelling tools, rulers, pulley blocks, bowls and wood engraving.

San Domingo Boxwood (58 lb.). This wood is sometimes used as a substitute for true boxwood. The heartwood has a yellow tinge, the sapwood is white to pale yellow. The texture is uniform and fine. It is very durable and has a straight but wavy grain. It carves well and takes a very high polish.

Butternut (27 lb.). The wood of the butternut, a member of the walnut family, is much in use for cabinetwork, inlay, and veneer as well as for carving. Unlike the walnut, however, this wood is soft and rather weak and may be carved entirely by hand. You should, in fact, avoid exerting too great an effort when working with this wood since, due to the weakness of its texture, you may easily make a larger cut than you had intended and thus ruin your project. A light grey-brown in color, butternut will take both paint and polish effectively.

Wild Cherry (40 lb.). Like other American fruit woods, wild cherry is a very good carving wood. It needs slow seasoning and tends to split if dried quickly. The sapwood is light and the heartwood a reddish brown. The texture is fine and even and it takes a smooth polish. It is used also in cabinet work, frames and other decorative work.

Sweet Chestnut (42 lb.). This wood can be mistaken for oak but it is about twenty-five per cent lighter when seasoned. The silver grain present in oak is absent, however. It is easy to work and has been widely used for timber work in churches.

Ebony (63 lb.). Ebony, not easily obtained, is black with a fine grain. The tools tend to blunt because of the rather gritty nature of the wood. It will take fine detail and a high polish.

Elm (36–37 lb.). Elm, like ash, is a wood familiar in everyday life. We see it in wheelbarrows, furniture and garden seats, and—like ash—it is tough and strong and suitable for large wood carvings.

Douglas Fir (31 lb.). This is a very strong wood and quite hard. It does, however, have a great tendency to check, split, shrink, and swell.

Holly (36 lb.). This wood, fine grained and heavy, is pure white in color. As the holly is of shrub-like proportions, its wood can be used, like boxwood, only for small objects and carvings, musical instruments, and inlay. Holly is fairly easy to work and will take detail without breaking or splitting.

Curly Jarrah (55 lb.). This wood is rich red in color and is probably the most important tree found in Western Australia. It can grow to as much as six feet in diameter. Jarrah carves well and takes a very high natural polish. It is extremely durable. The grain is straight but with a wavy or rippling character.

Iroko. This is the West African carver's favorite wood. Exposure to air turns the wood from straw color to red and the surface hardens. Finally, however, it becomes hard all through and it is resistant to termites.

Kingwood (70 lb.). This timber, not easily obtained, is found in Brazil and is similar to Indian Rosewood. Sizes are small, the maximum being 18 in. in diameter. The color of the wood is remarkable, almost violet with narrow, regular black stripes interspersed with wide, lighter bands. The grain is uniform and the wood will burnish to a fine natural polish.

Lignum Vitae (80-90 lb.). This is one of the heaviest of all woods and is therefore widely used for mallets and tools where weight and toughness is required. The heartwood is dark greenish brown and the sapwood a contrasting yellow. The fibres of the wood are interlocked and it is impossible to split, though it can be carved with sharp tools.

Lime (33 lb.). This is a favorite wood for sculpture. It is firm and pleasant to carve. The color is whitish to yellowish pink. Lime takes stain or bleach readily, the latter turning the timber pure white. It is moderately hard and takes a very good polish. Lime is also used for drawing boards, hat blocks and cabinetwork.

Honduras Mahogany (43 lb.). There are various species of mahogany, but from the carver's point of view the characteristics are similar. It is a good carving wood and of a beautiful rich red color. The grain is usually fairly straight. It does split rather easily and care must be taken in carving when this tendency is apparent. Mahogany glues well and takes a fine polish.

Red Maple (38 lb.). A wood with easy workability, red maple is used in woodenware, cabinetwork, and furniture.

Silver Maple (35 lb.). This soft maple is employed a great deal in trim and paneling.

Sugar Maple (42 lb.). This wood has a fine natural luster and is quite stable when properly dried.

Oak (43 lb.). For hundreds of years oak has been esteemed as one of America's finest woods. Although it is not eminently suited for small detail, it lends itself well to bold carving. It resembles ash and sweet chestnut in grain character.

Northern White Pine (25 lb.). Finely textured and of the usual yellow-white color of pine, this is an excellent wood for carving, because it is both easily worked and inexpensive.

Ponderosa Pine (28 lb.). This wood has a fine grain and finishes well. It is quite soft and of easy workability. It is a preferred material in paneling.

Sugar Pine (25 lb.). Like that of most pines, the wood of the sugar pine is a yellowish white in color, straight grained, and durable. A soft wood, it is easily carved by hand and will present no difficulties to the beginner. The grain of this pine is particularly stable and even.

Indian Rosewood (54 lb.). Rosewood is a rich, dark brown with dusky blackish markings and sometimes has a purplish tinge. It is hard and heavy and takes a very fine polish. It is excellent for carving but not inexpensive to buy. It is often used in the manufacture of musical instruments, billiard cues and fine inlay.

Eastern Spruce (28 lb.). A soft wood, with fair workability, it is especially favored for its soft and satiny texture. Although it is a strong wood, this spruce is not decay resistant. It is used particularly for making patterns and musical instruments.

Sycamore (40 lb.). Sycamore is white but turns light brown in the open air. It is very easy to carve. The grain is straight and indistinct. If used out of doors it should be protected against the weather as it rots very easily. It is fairly hard and is used for rollers, table tops, and textile machinery.

Teak (41 lb.). Teak is a rich golden brown. It carves readily but has a rather coarse and uneven texture. It is durable under almost any climatic conditions. The wood contains aromatic oils which act as a preservative. Its tough nature tends to blunt tools. The grain is straight but undulating—a quality peculiar to trees grown in dry soils. Teak is grown in India, Burma, and other countries of the Far East.

Black (American) Walnut (38 lb.). This wood of rich color and distinctive figure makes beautiful carvings for fine furniture, veneers, and cabinetwork. It is a hardwood.

Willow (30 lb.). Willow is straight grained, soft but tough. The wood is whitish to pale brown in the center. It seasons without difficulty and is suitable for carved toys.

Yew (46 lb.). Perhaps the most beautiful of the conifer woods. It is hard, with a fine decorative grain, excellent for wood carving, cabinetwork and turnery.

Procuring wood

With a little enterprise a small stock of wood suitable for carving can soon be acquired. Aim at collecting sound, dry timber. Visit large carpentry shops in your district where you may find that you can buy off-cuts for a few cents. Not all timber yards deal in seasoned woods, so inquire about this before buying. Large mahogany table legs from Victorian pieces may sometimes be found, also newel posts and thick wardrobe panels that can be utilized for carving in relief. If you are prepared to spend some money on a stock of wood and to buy seasoned timber, contact a firm dealing in a variety of woods, including hardwoods. Four inches is usually the maximum thickness of the planks supplied by such firms. These large merchants will not as a rule sell less than one plank which may be 9 or 10 ft. in length. If you do make this kind of investment, you will have enough wood to make a dozen or so small carvings. Do not despise the pines and firs which are often loosely termed 'deal'. Many of them have a very beautiful grain and can be polished if the grain of the wood is well sealed.

The grain of wood as it affects carving

The grain of wood has a bearing on carving in a visual sense and also in a practical way. In some woods, such as boxwood,

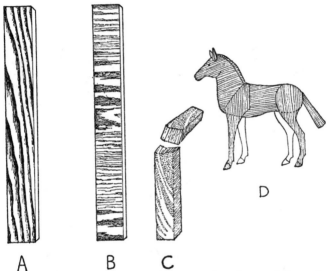

A   B   C

Fig. 5. Diagrams showing the strength and weakness of the grain. A. Tangential section in Douglas Fir. B. Cross-grain section in Douglas Fir. C. Cross-grain section in African Walnut. D. Structural use of grain in toys.

the grain is hardly visible and also tremendously strong, close, and even in texture. Other woods in this category are rosewood, ebony, and sycamore. In such woods fine detail can be cut in any direction without fear of a fracture. In figure 5, A, you will see a small piece of the 'tangential section in Douglas Fir, that is the grain fibres are running down the length of the section.

This gives strength. B shows a cross-section in the same wood:
this is weak and if a similar piece is less than 1 in. square
and 5 in. or more in length, it can be snapped very easily by
manual pressure. C is a drawing of a piece of black walnut
1 in. × ¾ in. × 5 in., and broken in the hand.

You should take care, therefore, to design your carving with
an eye to the direction of the grain. For instance, if you are carv-

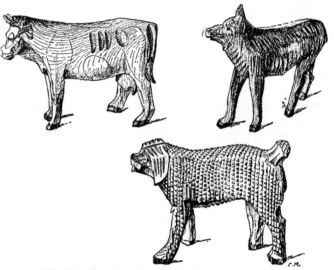

Fig. 6. Italian 'penny' toys; Yootha Rose collection.

ng an animal and the base, from one block, with the legs joined
to the body and base, they will be fairly strong even if the grain
runs across the legs. If, on the other hand, the legs are free without
a base, as in the Italian penny toys illustrated in figure 6, the grain
must run the length of the legs. These toys were sold in the Italian
markets during the 1920's and 30's for the equivalent of one penny.
If you look at them, you will notice that the necks are thick and
the noses rather short and the tail of the dog is at an angle. This

means that although carved from one piece, they are very strong. Only the cow's ears and horns are made of separate pieces of wood and glued in. These would certainly have broken off if carved from the main block. Cross-grain weakness is not confined to the softwoods. Hardwoods, such as oak, are very brittle in cross-section of less than $\frac{1}{2}$ in.

A diagonal run of grain is fairly strong and, as forms in carving do not necessarily run at right angles to each other, you are bound to find the grain running diagonally in many places. Also, the grain does twist and turn in some woods. In small work, such as toys, I would advise you to use close or straight grained wood with no knots, however small.

Ornament carvers, when making delicate carvings such as wall-light brackets, sometimes laminate sections with the grain of each piece running in the opposite direction to that of its neighbor. When glued up, these pieces support and strengthen each other. In figure 5, D, you see a method of making toys in eight sections for the sake of strength, the grain in every case running the length of the thinner parts of the horse; the ears, legs, tail and body are all in separate parts. This type of toy is usually cut out on a fret saw, glued up and then carved by a knife in the hand. I have used a similar method of construction in making a carved horse in mahogany for a restaurant sign. The pattern of the pieces will vary according to the design.

In many woods, such as jarrah, which grow under very dry conditions, the grain is often wavy but straight in direction. This type of grain in no way impedes carving. Woods such as lignum vitae, have an interlocking grain and turn well on a lathe but can be difficult for an inexperienced carver. In carving lime wood, apple, beech, cherry, sycamore, pine, oak, and mahogany, you will not find any serious difficulty as far as grain is concerned, provided you remember the strength and the weakness of wood described in this chapter.

Carving a log

In the previous chapter I have discussed the seasoning of wood and the desirability of using dry timber. There is a great risk of splitting if this latter rule is not observed. However, I do not overlook the fact that you may have a log of wood in your garden just asking to be carved. If you are willing to take a chance on its opening up then by all means go ahead. Cracks are not necessarily disastrous and can be filled. I have heard of carvings splitting completely in half but you may not be so unlucky. First bring the log under cover and jack it up on wood blocks in a cool dry place. If you can leave it for some months, do so. Many say that a log should be given a year's seasoning for every inch of its diameter. I have heard a timber merchant say that the center of a large log is never seasoned. It is not easy to make rules about this as so much depends on the type of wood and the humidity of the atmosphere. In any case you should not hasten the process of drying by exposing the log to direct heat. If you paint the cut ends it will help to prevent splitting. If a log is kept in the dark, in for instance the cellar, and then suddenly exposed to the light, splitting will often take place. I know this from painful experience.

In medieval times wood carvings were often made from the trunks of trees that had been hollowed out from the back. This enabled the wood to contract and expand. If, therefore, you hollow out the center of the log it will help. This is not easy but you can bore a few holes up through the center with the auger. This may prevent the star shakes shown in figure 4, F. In the oak carving by W. Soukop (PLATE XVI, page 56 ff.), the figure is built in sections and the center of the wood removed.

A carving in a large log of wood, such as elm, may develop cracks, but the wood is very tough and the whole mass holds together. When carving just to please yourself experiment with any wood available, remembering that most of the fruit woods are excellent for carving. Do not, therefore, turn your apple or cherry tree into logs for the fire.

CHAPTER THREE

The workshop or studio

IN wood carving it is possible to improvise by making a small working area in the corner of a living-room, that is if space is limited. If, on the other hand, you have a room or dry shed that can be used exclusively for carving, so much the better. Unlike stone carving, which creates a great deal of dust, wood carving can be termed a 'clean' craft as the dust is negligible and the wood chips can easily be swept up and burned. It is only when carving is combined with general carpentry and joinery that the complete workshop is absolutely necessary.

For carving, the first requirement is a really strong bench or table (PLATE I). A carpenter's bench will serve, or a stout kitchen table. If you use the latter, brace the legs with planks of wood at least 3 in. × 1 in., near floor level. Diagonal pieces can also be used for extra strength, but it may be best to get some advice first if you know nothing about carpentry. An average bench for carving is 5 ft. in length, 2 ft. to 2 ft. 6 in. in width and 3 ft. to 3 ft. 6 in. in height. Your own height should be considered. Working at a bench that is too low, carving can be a back-aching business. Arrange the height so that you can stand comfortably, or sit on a stool to work. It is advisable to have the bench top at least $1\frac{1}{2}$ in. to 2 in. thick. The bench must stand firmly on the floor and not move about as you work. A flimsy structure is useless. The bench can be used against a wall or standing free so that you have access to all sides. It really depends on the size and type of work in hand. Right-angled steel brackets can be used to anchor the bench to the wall or the floor. Place your bench in a good light as near a window as possible.

Gripping tools and fixing equipment

Although some wood carvers use little in the way of fixing equipment, most prefer to have their wood firmly held by cramps, bench screws or a vise. Very small work can be carved in the hand, very large work will hold steady by virtue of its own weight. In the case of work in the round, it is very useful to turn and move your work in order to get all views and to change the direction of cutting. Fixing equipment must be appropriate for the work in hand.

If you have acquired a carpenter's bench, it will in all probability have either a wood or iron bench vise attached to one side. This type of vise is very useful to the carver also. The metal bench vise can be bought at a hardware store and is fairly easy to fix, provided you have a stout bench designed to take it. The larger sizes are bolted to the bench, the smaller sizes screwed to the underside of the bench top which should be the same thickness as the depth of the jaws of the vise. This is in order that the jaws may close flush with the working surface of the bench. A rectangular recess should be cut in the bench to take the inner jaw so bringing it flush with the side of the bench top. It is important to fix wooden cheeks to the jaws of an iron vise in order to prevent bruising on your carving. Holes are usually already drilled in the jaws for this purpose. As sizes and types differ you should get some information regarding fixing at the time of purchase.

The wood carver's vise (Fig. 7, E)

This is a most useful tool for the amateur as it is easy to fix on any improvised bench. It is attached by a heavy screw that passes down through a hole in the bench. The vise is drawn tight to the bench by a wing-nut underneath. In order not to split or damage the bench top, a piece of wood should be drilled and used as a washer before screwing on the wing-nut. Both screw and nut are provided with the vise. The jaws are fitted with cork and leather buffs, an added protection, and particularly useful when the wood is very soft or the work delicate.

The bench holdfast (Fig. 7, D)

This tool needs no fixing. The shaft is inserted in a hole in the bench and the foot rests on the carving. When the screw is turned

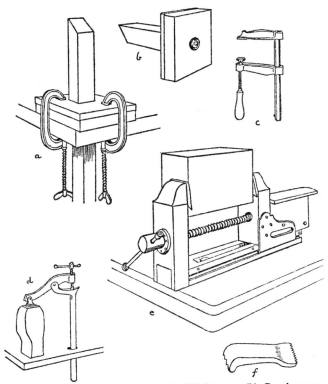

Fig. 7. Tools to hold the carving. (a) 'G' Cramps. (b) Coach screw. (c) Screw cramp. (d) Bench holdfast. (e) Wood carver's vise. (f) Metal clips for holding relief used in pairs.

the work is held firm by the pressure of the shaft on the side of the hole. The principle of the holdfast seems surprisingly simple but it is nevertheless efficient. It should be used on a bench top not less than 2 in. thick.

The carver's bench screw (Fig. 8, A)

To use the carver's bench screw a hole must be drilled in the

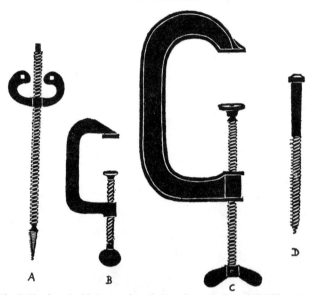

Fig. 8. Tools to hold the carving. A. Bench screw. B and C. 'G' cramps.
D. Coach screw.

bench. The pointed end is screwed into the block to be carved
and tightened by a wing-nut under the bench. As with the carver's
vise, a block of wood should be used as a washer (Fig. 9). By

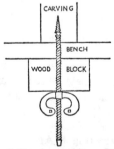

Fig. 9. Bench screw in position.

varying the size of this block you can lengthen or shorten the screw.

Coach screws (Fig. 8, D)

The coach screw can be used for fixing the carving in the same manner as the bench screw. Coach screws are also invaluable for fixing one heavy piece of wood to another. For instance, the large figure illustrated in PLATE XII is held to the cross by coach screws. A tall block, as shown in figure 7, B, can be firmly held by a 6 in. or 8 in. coach screw. Short screws will work loose with the continual vibration of the mallet. Large hardware dealers will supply them up to 8 in. in length and $\frac{3}{8}$ in. or $\frac{1}{2}$ in. thick. Holes must be drilled to take the coach screws and tightening is done by means of a spanner.

'G' cramps (Fig. 7, A and Fig. 8, C)

The 'G' cramp is obtainable in many sizes and is useful in all kinds of woodwork, including wood carving. The type with the swivel shoe is best for the carver as it will tighten on surfaces that are not parallel. For secure fixing use them in pairs.

The screw cramp (Fig. 7, C)

This is of German design and used in the same way as the 'G' cramp.

Sash cramps

These range in length from 3 ft. to 6 ft. and are used by joiners for assembling frames. For this reason the jaws are only 2 in. or 3 in. long. The carver will find them useful in gluing up large work if he uses them in pairs with a stout board on each side of his work. In figure 10 the arms of a figure are being glued up at the shoulders.

The sloping stand or table (Figs. 11 and 12)

With the help and advice of friends I have recently evolved this piece of equipment and have found it excellent for carving

B

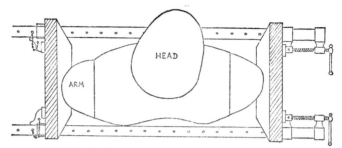

Fig. 10. Sash cramps in use; gluing arms at shoulder.

Fig. 11. The sloping stand: front view.

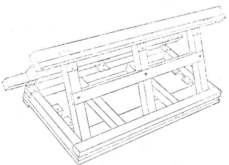

Fig. 12. The sloping stand: back view.

both wood and stone panels. For anyone with a little knowledge of carpentry it is a fairly simple piece of construction. The framework is made of wood 2 in. × 2 in. and the main board is 36 in. × 16 in. The whole stand could be made smaller or larger, according to your own requirements. You will see from the picture of the back view illustrated that the stand is adjustable on the deck-chair principle. This particular model can be used at three different angles. The hinges on the supporting frame should be of a heavy type and not less than 2 in. in width as they will have to stand up to a good deal of vibration. The wood of the main board should be at least 1 in. in thickness. The wood to be carved can be fixed on by bench screws, 'G' cramps, or by ordinary screws. This stand can be easily bolted down to the bench. The advantage of a sloping stand is that you can stand upright to carve and step back to see your work.

Other methods of fixing a panel

If you want your work flat on the bench, and many carvers do, it is an easy matter to fix the panel. Bench screws can be used (see Fig. 9). The length of these can be varied by interposing a block of wood between the wing-nut and the underside of the bench. You can also fix a frame of wood around your carving and drive in a few wooden wedges to hold it tight (Fig. 37). If you are working on a fairly heavy piece of wood, two wood stops screwed down at right angles to each other will be sufficient.

CHAPTER FOUR

Tools

THE wood carver uses a number of carpenter's tools at various stages in his work. In a few cases the carver and carpenter use tools of the same name, but very different in type. For instance, the carpenter's mallet is a modified rectangular block while the carver's mallet is round in section with a much shorter handle. The carpenter's gouge is thick and heavy by comparison to a carver's. When carving, use the carver's tools. An initial interest in carpentry will often develop into a wish to carve and some knowledge of woodwork and joinery is very valuable to the carver.

Primitive tools

As carving is a natural activity of man, children at an early age will start to whittle sticks and carve with a pen-knife. Many country people who do not pretend to be carvers will cut an ash cane from the hedge. The bent root is used as the handle which they will proceed to carve into the form of an animal or bird. I often saw such sticks made by my father. Round-headed nails were used for eyes. These root-carved hybrids, half accident and half contrived, had a very special fascination for us as children.

In historical museums there are examples of flint knives, chisels and even gouges dating from Neolithic times. The knife is still a favorite tool for toy makers and for small work carved in the hand. As work increases in size, carving with the knife becomes impracticable. Chopping and striking tools like the axe and the adze also have primitive origins, and they are still used today in the timber trade and to a limited extent by the carver. The African can complete a carving by means of the adze, using a variety of blades that can be interchanged in the same handle. I have also seen it used very skilfully in carving the large type of rocking horse.

36

Shaping and shaving tools such as the draw knife and spoke-shave, although primarily wheelwright's tools, can be of use in carving. This overlapping in the use of tools in different trades is not surprising when in every case the basic material is the same, namely timber.

THE FIRST KIT OF TOOLS

Carving tools are expensive and the beginner need not make a large outlay at first. The following list is the minimum required.

A bench
1 mallet, 2 lb.
2 8 in. 'G' cramps
4 gouges
1 fluter or veiner
A tin of cycle oil
1 Carborundum stone
(coarse and medium combined)
1 fine India or Washita stone
3 slipstones to fit the gouges
A leather strop

The wood carver will inevitably need some general woodworking tools. The following list is in order of likely necessity.

Hand or cross-cut saw, 26 in.
Tenon saw, 14 in.
Screwdriver, 8 in. blade
Brace and bits
Rose countersink bit
Hand brace
Try square, 12 in.
Steel rule
Bow saw
Wing compasses

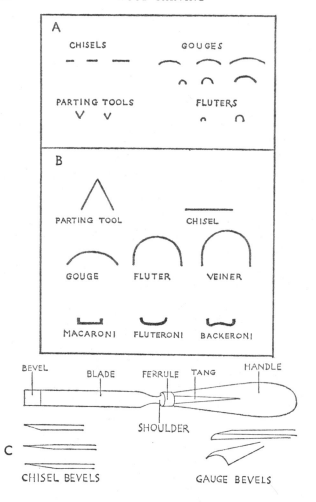

Fig. 13. Tool sections. A. Selection of suitable tools for the beginner. B. Carving tools, sections of the main types. C. Bevels.

The carver's mallet (Fig. 14)

The round, short-handled mallet is indispensable. One of medium weight, e.g. 2 lb., will enable you to start. If you can also buy two more, one light and one heavy, so much the better. Remember that the mallet, in view of its weight, is doing a part of the work for you. If you are unaccustomed to this type of tool, your wrist may complain at first, but gradually it will get stronger. When there is pain in the wrist, it is best to give it a rest or use a

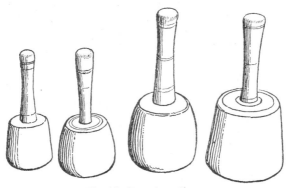

Fig. 14. Carver's mallets.

lighter mallet. The lighter mallet also gives you greater flexibility for delicate work. The heavy mallet should be used on large work and saves time and energy in roughing out. You will find that, with practice, you need not grip the mallet tightly all the time but can loosen the grip slightly on impact with the tool. This method takes the jar out of the blow and makes the whole process less tiring.

Mallets are made in a number of woods chosen for their toughness and weight. Beech and lignum vitae are the most commonly used. The latter, apart from snakewood, is the heaviest known wood and easy to recognize by the marked difference between the yellow sapwood and almost black heartwood. Do not misuse your mallet by bruising it on metal. The stone mason does use a wooden mallet on steel tools but that is another story. The Dummy mallet is favored by some carvers; it has the advantage of being heavy but small. Sometimes the professional wood carver uses his hand as a mallet (PLATE II).

The gouge

The gouge and its near relations the fluter and veiner are the carver's most valuable cutting tools. There are hundreds of sizes and types, varying in depth of curve and ranging in size from

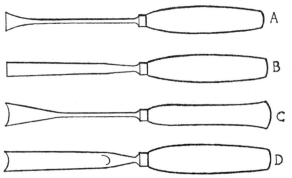

Fig. 15. Tool shapes: gouges and chisels. A. Spade chisel. B. Straight-shafted chisel. C. Spade-shaped gouge. D. Straight-shafted gouge.

2 in. to ⅛ in. There are also those with back bends and curved shafts for easier cutting on concave surfaces and the twisting undercuts in ornament carving. For general purposes, and moderate sized carvings, tools ranging from ⅛ in. to ¾ in. will suffice. Eight good tools will enable you to start work. Should you have the opportunity of buying secondhand tools, take it at once. I have been fortunate in this way a number of times. These tools may be fifty or so years old, and are likely to have belonged to some craftsman who cared for them. Such 'broken in' tools are delightful to use, often made with finely shaped handles and well tempered steel. You will notice that in the first kit of tools I have

suggested a medium or shallow curve in each gouge. When using a gouge with a very deep curve, you may tend to cut too deeply. Remember that the surface of the form is at the base of the cut. The spade gouge (Fig. 15) has the advantage of being light and pleasant to use.

SHARPENING AND GRINDING TOOLS

Bevels. The carpenter's firmer chisel is made for chopping dovetail joints and for work of a similar kind. He uses other types for paring and mortising, and he uses gouges for mouldings. These tools are, as I have pointed out, very different from the carver's. The bevel of carpenter's chisels for average work is about 25 degrees; it is also flat and sharpened on one side only. The carver's chisel, on the other hand, may have a bevel of 10 degrees, or even less on small tools, and is bevelled on both sides. The carver does the bulk of his work with the gouge and the bevel required here is curved. This is easy to understand for carving has a flowing motion, the gouge penetrating the wood but returning to the surface continually.

The bevel on a new carving tool may be too steep and may need reducing to 15 degrees or less. This can be done on the coarser type of oilstone. A steep bevel impedes progress in carving. The bevel on a gouge need have no upper edge and can curve gently to the sides of the shaft. When pushing by hand, the tool pivots on the rounded bevel and is easy and flexible to use. The carving tool in use develops a smooth and polished back.

Try to keep your tools in good condition. Wipe them over occasionally with an oily rag when they are not in use to keep them free from rust. Do not allow them to blunt each other by throwing them carelessly into a drawer. You can keep them separate by using divisions in a box, or sewn divisions in a baize roll, or by hanging them on a rack. A professional wood carver may have dozens of tools on his bench but he gets the habit of putting each one down in a way that will not damage the cutting edge.

It is almost impossible to exaggerate the importance of having sharp tools for carving. The amateur will not find sharpening easy at first but success will come with perseverance. Much time may have to be given to the process before you have a set of really useful tools. When you buy carving tools, they are roughly ground but not sharpened. For sharpening them you will need at least two oilstones (Fig. 16c), a number of different sized slipstones (Fig. 16a), oil and a leather strop.

Fig. 16. (a) Slipstones. (b) Using the slipstone. (c) Oilstone.

Oilstones can be divided into natural and manufactured stones. India and Carborundum belong to the latter group. The natural stones, such as Washita and Arkansas, have a slower action but give a finer edge. Commence sharpening a new tool with Carborundum and finish on slower stones. Dalmore stone can also be used at the early stages of sharpening. It is possible to buy Carborundum in two grades on one stone: coarse on one side and medium or fine on the other. A stone 8 in. in length is a good size for most purposes. The finishing stone, such as Washita or Arkansas, can be smaller. Arkansas, a fine white stone, is expensive but excellent for giving the tool a final edge before stropping.

Slipstones, made of the same materials as oilstones, have rounded and shaped edges for sharpening the inside of gouges, veiners, fluters and parting tools. The kidney slipstone is tapered and can be used on tools of varying sizes.

A wooden frame can be tacked on the bench to prevent the oilstone from moving about while it is being used. The leather strop can also be tacked to the bench on a board. Oilstones will last for years if well looked after. Small chisels can be sharpened on the side of the stone so as to save wear on the broad surface. The oilstone should be flat at all times. If the surface becomes uneven, rub it down on a sheet of coarse emery cloth. Place the emery cloth on a really flat surface. A thick piece of glass is ideal.

Oil. A fine machine or cycle oil is quite satisfactory. Never use linseed oil as this will make the stone unusable. It hardens and clogs the stone. If you have made this mistake, you can redeem it by heating the stone gently in water and washing soda. For ordinary cleaning, soak the stone in paraffin and scrub with a stiff brush. It will not be necessary to do this very often provided you wipe the stone clean after use with a soft rag. A stone needs cleaning when it becomes glazed and loses cutting power.

The leather strop. This will give your tools the final razor edge. Very fine abrasives such as pumice or emery paste can be used on this. A small piece of leather can be used round the finger for the inside of the gouges.

Sharpening the gouge

There are a number of schools of thought as regards methods of sharpening. I will describe most fully the method I use myself. There is no doubt that different ways suit different people and various types of work.

Sculptors usually sharpen tools with the oilstone on the bench. This is the method I use myself, and is, I think, the easiest way for the amateur. Put a few drops of oil on the stone. Hold the tool in the right hand. Place the fingers of the left hand on the shaft, as shown in PLATE VII. Start slowly, keeping the angle low and the pressure even. Do not change the angle. Move the tool from side to side on the stone while at the same time twisting the right wrist. By this motion you will ensure that all parts of the curved edge of the tool can reach the stone. But be careful not to take the outside corners off the edge. Keep testing the edge by gently drawing your thumb across it. You should also hold the tool to the light. If you can see the edge, the tool is still blunt. You may see it in one place only; if so, then give this part extra attention. If you now feel the inside edge, you will notice that a slight burr has formed. Take this off with a slipstone that fits the curve. Hold the slipstone in the hand and rub it against the tool. Keep the angle low. Now draw the tool briskly along the strop, keeping the blade almost flat. The tool should now be ready for use. Test it on a piece of wood.

Another method. It is a common practice among cabinet makers and professional wood carvers to sharpen the gouge as follows. The tool is held in the left hand, the elbow crooked with the handle against the side of the body. The stone is oiled and held in the right hand and rubbed up and down against the bevel of the gouge, the inside of the curve facing the operator and the stone behind the tool. At the same time, the blade is rolled in the fingers of the left hand, the edge so contacting the stone at all points. A lightweight stone is used, often the side of a slipstone. The burr is taken off in the manner already described. This may well be one of the best ways of sharpening a gouge but it needs a lot of practice and before trying it I advise you to watch a demonstration by an expert.

Sharpening the carver's chisel

Put a few drops of oil on the stone. Stand facing the short end of the stone. Rub the tool up and down the length of the stone, keeping the angle steady and the pressure even. Look at the polish on the bevel to see if the whole width is making proper contact. Repeat on the other side. As I have already pointed out, for carving, the angle of the bevel should not, as a rule, be more than 15 degrees, and can be less. It is useful to have varying types. Some very useful spade chisels are very slim in section, with angles that resemble a knife-blade. If the chisel is bevelled on one side only, sharpen this side as described above. Turn the tool over, hold it flat on the stone, rub a few times. This will loosen the burr. Reverse again, using your fine oilstone. Place the tool at the end of the stone. Do not use much pressure. Draw the tool toward you. This will push the burr back from the edge. Repeat on the other side, keeping the tool flat on the stone. Repeat these movements until the edge is clean. Finish all chisels on the strop. The edge, if sharp, should now be invisible when held against the light.

The methods described can be adapted to the sharpening of all other carving tools. Back-bent and deeply curved tools need extra care and patience. Wipe the tools clean before you start carving. Oil makes a penetrating stain on wood.

Grinding and grinding stones

A new carving tool is only roughly ground. If you have no grindstone, the Carborundum oilstone will serve. The process of grinding will be slower but equally efficient. In the case of the gouge, work on the bevel until you have obtained the right angle. This may take time and really hard rubbing. See that the edge is straight. If it is not, correct it before you start grinding by the method described in the paragraph on damaged tools.

Although the grindstone need not be considered an absolute necessity for the beginner, it is very useful to possess one when tools are damaged or worn. At the same time, a tool can be very easily spoiled beyond repair if the grindstone is badly used. Water is an essential part of grinding to prevent overheating in the metal. Grindstones are usually fitted with a water trough for this purpose. Before investing in a grindstone, a demonstration of its proper use is advisable. Some are operated by hand, and these need a second operator to turn the handle. The grindstone operated by the feet leaves both hands free to hold the tool and is convenient for the carver working alone.

Damaged tools

If your tools have nicks, wavy edges or any faults of this kind, they must be attended to before sharpening proper begins. If you have no grindstone, you can straighten the edge by rubbing it down on medium Carborundum with a blunting action, holding the tool at right angles to the stone and pressing firmly as you rub in one direction, using oil. Look at the edge. It may be straight but of uneven thickness. This can be remedied by the usual sharpening action on one of your coarser stones, giving the thick parts of the edge extra rubbing. Examine the edge continually until it appears as a thin, even line. Continue sharpening with a finer stone, and then strop.

USING THE GOUGE

As the types and shapes of the gouge can be numbered in hundreds, uses also are many and varied. Although for a carving in the round one or two can suffice, it is in the more complicated forms of relief and ornament carving that it is just as well to have a good selection. In the first stages of such carving and after the design is drawn on the wood, the gouge is often used in a chopping action, the tool being held in an almost vertical position. The curve of the gouge is selected to fit the curves of the drawing, the tool being driven into the wood almost at right angles. Cutting tools should be used in this way when establishing the design of a relief or cutting shallow detail on a work in the round. It is in fact equivalent to drawing. However, when you are roughing out or carving in the round do not drive the gouge in too deep. By doing so the gouge can get stuck or broken as you try to get it out. A safe method in this case is to let one corner of the cutting edge remain visible; often both corners are above the surface of the wood.

Hand-pushing the gouge

The hand-pushing of tools (PLATE X) plays a major part in wood carving. A skilled carver pushes, twists and is in a sense drawing the form as he cuts. This kind of skill takes time to perfect but you should practice using the tool in this way, and the tool must be razor sharp. The left hand that holds the shaft of the tool must rest on the carving and act like a brake. The tool is therefore in perfect control. Hand-pushing can be dangerous if this latter rule is not observed.

Fixing handles

As handles are usually sold separately you may be obliged to fix it to the blade yourself. The following method is quite simple. Wrap the blade in a protective cloth and put it in a vise with only the shoulder protruding. You will find that the handle has a small hole drilled in the end but it will not be large enough to take the tang. Press the end of the tang into this hole and holding the handle firmly twist it back and forth. By this method the tang acts as a drill. When the hole is long enough for the tang to enter the handle to within an inch of the shoulder, tap the handle home with the mallet. The thick square end of the tang will hold the blade firm in the handle.

ABRASIVE TOOLS

Although abrasive tools are widely used in conjunction with wood carving, they can do more harm than good if used thoughtlessly. Train yourself, at first, to do without these aids. You will make a much better carver if you rely on the sharp edge of your gouge and chisel.

Shaping tools

Tools such as the rasp have a long line of ancestors but the Surform tool with removable blade is a comparatively new arrival and has proved to be a very useful tool for the amateur woodworker. This type of tool has to some extent replaced the rasp. It has the advantage of a smooth cut combined with rapid cutting action. The blades are flexible and I have used them at times without the frame. The blade is held in both hands and slightly bent while working. It is, however, brittle and should not be bent too much or it will snap. For large surfaces it is best to use the blades in their proper frames. These tools can be obtained in a number of shapes and sizes.

The rasp

The medium and smaller sizes are of most use to the wood carver. Very large rasps with heavy teeth need arduous labor to be really effective. The rasp should not be used near the finished surface of the carving as the scoring marks can go fairly deep. It can be most useful on large works, for 'pulling together' shapes that are too vague, for shaping sweeping convex or concave forms, for establishing a plane and opening the way to further cutting with the gouge. Used without thought, the rasp can weaken form or make the work dull and soft in character.

Rifflers (Fig. 17)

The riffler is a type of rasp which can be bought in all shapes and sizes and is therefore useful in awkward corners and for removing wood from inaccessible places. The riffler, like the rasp, has a fraying action on the wood. Again it must be pointed out that normally it is better to cut the wood. It is all too easy for the amateur to turn to rasps and rifflers when tools are blunt or a little extra skill is required.

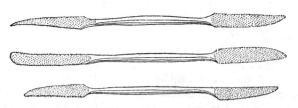

Fig. 17. Rifflers.

Plate I. *Above:* Wood carver's home-made bench. *Plate II. Below left:* Mr Harold Board carving panels for the House of Commons using his hand as a mallet. *Plate III. Below right:* The late Mr A. G. Cole carving a remembrance stand in oak.

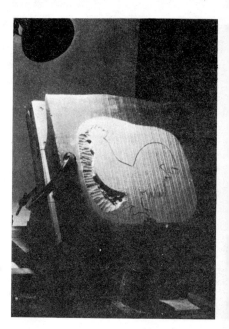

Plate IV. Above left: Tool rack. *Plate V. Right:* Cockerel; commencement of carving in lime wood. *Plate VI. Below left:* Indian high relief, nineteenth century; Yootha Rose collection. *Plate VII. Right:* Sharpening a gouge.

'The Risen Christ in Glory': *Plate VIII. Above left:* The glued-up block. *Plate IX. Right:* Using calipers on the carving. *Plate X. Below left:* Pushing the gouge by hand. *Plate XI. Right:* Further stage of carving.

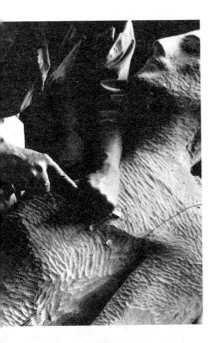

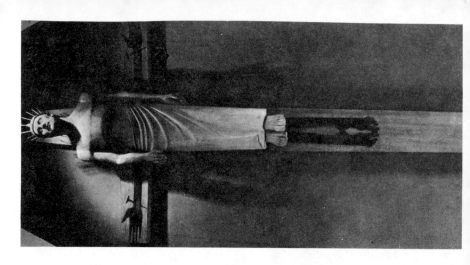

Plate XII. Above: 'The Risen Christ in Glory' in lime wood; figure 8 ft. 6 in., cross 16 ft., by Freda Skinner, St. Paul's, Lorrimore Square, London, S.E.17.
Plate XIII. Below: Detail of head.

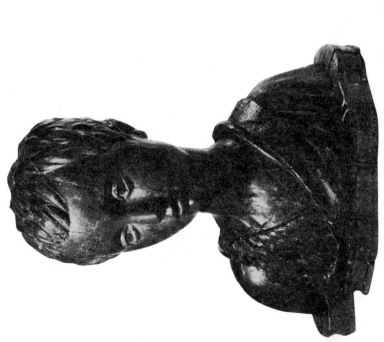

Plate XIV. Left: Italian Renaissance, school of Rosselino, 'Head of St. John the Baptist', owned by Trinity College, Oxford, exhibited at the Ashmolean Museum. *Plate XV. Right*: Carved Dish in oak, 25½ in. by 12¾ in. by 1½ in., by David Pye.

Plate XVI. Left: 'Fisher Girl' in oak, 4 ft. 4 in. by Willi Soukop, 1952.
Plate XVII. Right: 'Internal and External Forms', elmwood, 8 ft. 7 in., by
Henry Moore, 1953/4, Albright Art Gallery, Buffalo, N.Y.

Plate XVIII. Above: Method of carving applied decoration; Harold Board's workshop. Plate XIX. Below: 'Cat with Fish', ebony, by Elizabeth Spurr; J. M. Paynton collection.

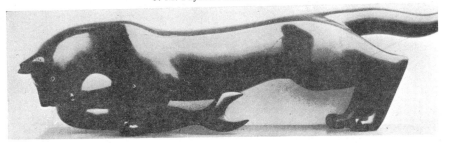

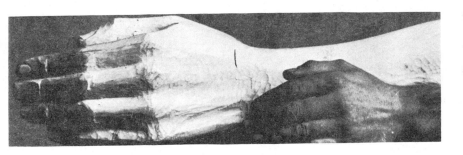

Plate XX. Above: A carved hand. Plate XXI. Below: Copy of eighteenth-century mantelpiece in pine by Harold Board.

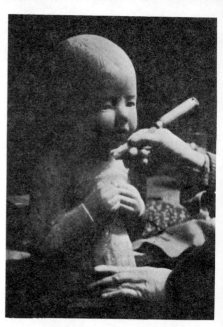

Plate XXII. Above left: 'Knight and Lady', fourteenth century, Clifton Reynes, England.

Plate XXIII. Above: 'Christopher' in pearwood, by Polly Hill Clarke.

Plate XXIV. Left: 'Wolf's Head', totem pole, elmwood, by John Linfield.

Scrapers

The scraper is not often used by the carver. However, a small 1 in. scraper set in a handle can sometimes be useful for cleaning out the flat background of a high relief. It is held at a high angle to the work and used with a scraping action. A chisel can be adapted for this purpose. Frequent re-sharpening is necessary as the scraping has a blunting action on the tool. Do not resort to scraping if the wood can be carved in one of the usual ways.

Sandpaper

When using sandpaper, get a supply of all grades. Do not use the paper across the fibres of the grain as this will scar the wood and the scratches are very difficult to eradicate. Try to work with the grain, using the finest grades for finishing. The smooth finish given by sandpaper is suitable for rounded forms, flat surfaces, and for woods where the maximum amount of grain figure is desired. Used indiscriminately, sandpaper can blur small forms and take the sharpness from the detail. Remember that making a shape smooth does not automatically make the shape a good one. If what you intend is to give your carving a smooth finish, go all out for this. Tool-cuts with their edges just blurred over by sandpaper will give a very unpleasant result.

CHAPTER FIVE

General advice for the amateur

WHEN the workshop is prepared try a few simple exercises described in chapter 6 so that you may acquire practice with tools and get to know the 'feel' of the wood. You will then be ready to think of designing something yourself, and before doing so, look at some really good wood carvings. Photographs can remind us of things seen but for proper appreciation it is better to see the actual work. A visit to the local museum is a good idea, or to a church or building where fine wood carvings can be seen. Grinling Gibbons, the English sculptor, was one of the most skilful wood carvers who ever lived and for the realistic carving of natural form in wood he is unsurpassed. (Fig. 18).

There is no harm in borrowing ideas from the richest sources. This has always happened as a natural evolution in the arts. It would be absurd to say that the artist must always endeavour to copy natural forms, but rather that in nature we have a field of inspiration and profitable study. If for instance, we use the human figure, or animal form in design, we are engaged in a translation from flesh to wood, stone, or paint, from life movement to movement in a static material. We can find pattern motives in such natural forms as shells and leaves. The African carver finds many of his patterns in the skins of snakes. We draw our ideas then from works of the present and the past and also from life. Even visionary artists such as Willliam Blake did not find the image of their designs without the influence of environment and the work of other artists.

The amateur should not be discouraged by all the tools, methods, diagrams and equipment discussed in this book. It may appear at a glance that the business of wood carving is too involved or costly. I must therefore point out at once that you can carve if you have a piece of wood, a kitchen table, three gouges, and two 'G' cramps. Many of us in the profession have a magpie acquisitiveness where tools are concerned and like to be

Fig. 18. Carving in lime wood by Grinling Gibbons, Belton House, Grantham, England.

equipped for all eventualities. This is quite unnecessary for someone who intends to carve occasionally. Indeed, some well-known highly successful wood carvers manage perfectly well with very simple equipment and prefer to do so. So much depends on the work in hand. As you progress you will naturally wish to buy more tools from time to time but this can be a gradual process.

Do not try to copy an ivory or metal object as the designs may be unsuitable for wood. Do not expect to be able to carve with the skill of a Chinese ivory carver who has been doing it all his life. For the amateur, time is no object and patience is essential. If you have an idea that comprises two or more figures, it may be better to try a high relief rather than attempt it in the round. Read first the chapters on equipment and sharpening tools, then the paragraph on procuring wood. Start with a wood of medium hardness such as lime. You may be discouraged if you commence with a hardwood such as oak. Very soft woods can also be difficult, needing razor sharp tools and skill in carving, and you may find that you are cutting away too much, too soon. Soft woods also tend to blunt tools quickly. If, however, you are working under the supervision of a teacher it is quite another matter as you will then get guidance in carving and help in sharpening your tools. Not all art schools specialize in wood carving and it is best to inquire locally if you wish to attend classes.

Do not try to work too small at first. It is easier to work on broad surfaces and will also make you bolder and more fearless in the way you use the tools. A complete figure may be too difficult if you have no experience in drawing. A head or an animal would be less of a problem. If you are interested in ornament, you could pick a leaf from the garden and use it as a basis for a design. In leaves you can find simple shapes with infinite variety. When you have carved one simple piece well it is easy to advance to something more difficult.

Design

If you are very eager to try a figure, it will do no harm to look at primitive and peasant carving. Look at the American Indian carving illustrated in figure 19. Here you will see a draped figure in most simple terms. This would be a starting point. Carve the body and head as one uniform statement. In the work of early civilizations and more primitive communities there is a zest and simplicity far away from naturalism. There is also a great feeling for pattern and design. It is interesting to make a near copy of something you admire but you will not wish to continue working in a manner that belongs to other countries and civilizations. Therefore, it is better to learn from them but gradually begin to make your own designs.

You can try out texture and pattern with your different

Fig. 19. *Indian Woman*, painted wood, Vancouver Island, Canada.

tools and master the use of them before starting on a definite project. It is often easier for the beginner to visualize his design as a profile or silhouette. If you are working in relief, an outline is enough to work from. You will discover how to develop this in the process of cutting. If you wish to carve an animal in the round, read the chapter on carving a pigeon. Even if you prefer to carve some other object of simple design, the principles described can be adapted and will still hold good.

You may have a smooth-haired cat in the house, if so, you have a model ready at hand. You may at first see your cat's head as a round knob with fur on it but as you look closer, you will observe that the shape is full of variety, of flat planes and curves that lend themselves to carving. Try to discriminate when you are looking at other models or carvings of animals. Avoid the sentimental approach or you will lose the real character and vigor of the animal. Look, for instance, at the way the Egyptians carved their sacred cats in wood and in stone. Observe that the sweet little pottery deer, with eyes six times too large, is no relation of the beautiful animal you can see for yourself in the parks and zoos. If you have no confidence in your drawing but feel you can carve a shape then just make diagrammatical drawings as a shorthand for yourself. If you can get the habit of looking at live things with the idea of using them in your carvings you will begin to see forms and shapes in relation to one another. Notice, for instance, the size of the head. A small head on a figure or animal will make the body look large. A large head on your cat will turn it into a kitten.

If you feel incapable of designing your own carving, be careful from what source you get your inspiration. If you are going to copy ornament, try to work from the photograph or drawing of an original piece belonging to the period in which it was carved. At first it may be difficult to appreciate the reason why so many modern copies of Gothic ornament become deadly dull. It is as though the wine had been watered down too many times and the original flavor destroyed. It is also that a 'tidying up' process goes on. The parts of the design are measured and all made symmetrical. The medieval carver let his work grow more naturally. In consequence his leaves and flowers are still living while the copies are dead. There is more to a work of art than its obvious exterior, and something copied just 'as a job' cannot have the life infused into it as when the design was first carved, say, in the fourteenth century with feeling and a sense of adventure. If, on the other hand, you contemplate some early piece of carving with real appreciation and great liking you may be able to make use of this design and carve something which is in part your own. You must not only be in love with the action of carving but also with your own idea about it. Therefore, before you shut yourself in your workshop go out and look at living things and works of art.

It is interesting to compare similar subjects carved in wood and stone, or modelled for bronze. When bronze has been worked on with tools and files after casting, it has something in common with carving. I have advised you to get ideas for wood carving from the works in that material. However, examples as the animal sculptures in bronze, page 153, and the stone carving from Notre Dame in Paris, page 155, can be a source of inspiration to those looking for ideas. As you become more familiar with wood carving, you will recognize forms that can be translated from stone or bronze to a carving in wood.

Structure in design

If we accept that good design springs from an appreciation and some understanding of organic form, some acquaintance with structure in plants and animals will be of real value to the carver. The sculptor is often primarily concerned with the human form but, as we have already seen, there are many less complex living forms that can aid and inspire design.

The structure of a building is first apparent in the scaffolding. In animal life, bones are the scaffolding. In the skeleton we have the key to proportion, articulation, movement, balance and scale. The importance of these things cannot be over-estimated. The reader may never have attended an art school or looked at an anatomy book and the structure of muscle and bone is a highly complicated affair. Do not let this deter you in your attempts to design, but it must be remembered that muscles, features and fur are all controlled in shape by the bone-structure. In the diagrams of simplified skeleton shapes, the bone-structure of animals is indicated. It will help you if you notice the points where the bone is almost on the surface of the form, e.g. the skull, shoulders, spine and at the joints. The inability to draw in a realistic way can be partially overcome if you plot these points in making your design.

Whenever possible this should be allied with observation and drawing of the living animal. The skeleton diagrams in no way indicate the full anatomy and are only intended as a guide

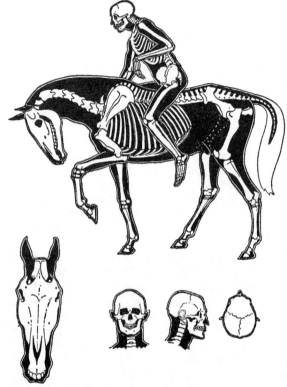

Fig. 20. Skeleton diagrams: man and horse (drawing by James Turner).

to right thinking and planning of animal shape. There are great pitfalls for the beginner as forms not based on structure can be weak, dull and repetitive. In a limited way, the amateur can

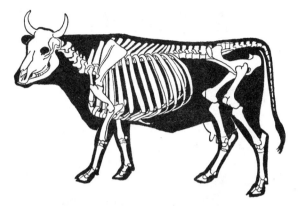

Fig. 21. Skeleton diagram of a cow.

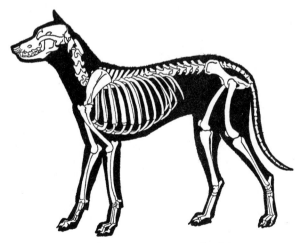

Fig. 22. Skeleton diagram of a dog.

begin to design his carving, but he must start with fundamentals. If you are a beginner, remember that 'fools rush in', pause to think, and start with structure.

Design and carving progress together

It should be obvious from what I have said, that you must be interested in the shape of your carving from the very beginning.

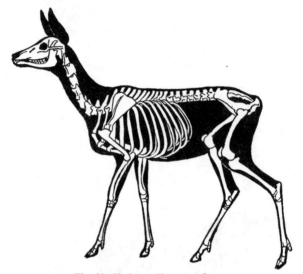

Fig. 23. Skeleton diagram of a roe.

During the first stages of carving you may have something resembling a snowman, but you are from the outset experimenting with form. You must give yourself your own limits of expression. Through the ages there have been wide deviations from the literal presentation of natural form. This is legitimate and modern artists go very far in this direction. With experience an artist will know what weakens or strengthens, and selects by instinct. A very abstract design may well have its roots in organic form and will be all the better for that. Consistency is something that should be aimed for, I think, in treatment of the carving. If it is a very long and thin figure, then the arms and head must be in

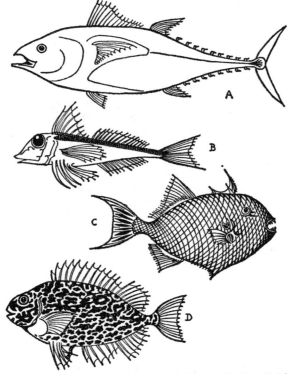

Fig. 24. Fish shapes. A. Short-Finned Tunny. B. Sea Robin.
C. Trigger Fish. D. Siganid.

character with your conception of the whole. At the same time, do not allow monotony of form to creep into your work.

When carving a figure in the round try to think in terms of sections and not only in silhouette. Take for instance the arm.

Look at your own arm in the mirror. It could be treated as a cylinder, the same width all the way down, but this would be a dull form. A tapering cylinder would be nearer the truth and more interesting. Look at your arm again and you will see how the cylinder is modified by flatter facets at the wrists and inside the upper arm. You will see swift curves on the lower arm terminating in the fine straight lines in the bones of the hand. Notice how the forms twist with the movement of the hand. Movement is something we must consider here. This does not necessarily mean movement of an active kind, as for instance a running figure. Look for movement in the shapes. For instance, a figure can be said to have movement if the weight is on one leg, one knee is bent and the head turned. In the case of an animal, movement may be introduced into the flexible spine. Do not value symmetry too much. In nature one side of a head is never exactly like the other.

As you carve do not attempt to finish one part but keep the whole design as far as possible at the same stage. This is very important, particularly at the beginning. The amateur is over-anxious to see the end-product quickly and usually gets too interested in the face and tries to carve this long before the shape of the head as a whole has been established. Keep the head large at first because the features and line of profile need a fair amount of wood. On the other hand, do not be hypnotized by the idea 'I must not take off too much, I cannot put it back'. If you know that the shoulders must be lowered two inches in order to get a head and neck then cut the spare wood away without hesitation.

One of the difficulties for the beginner is to form a clear idea of the completed work. Therefore, do not be too ambitious at first and stick to your idea. It is far better to complete the first carving and if you are not satisfied, then do another. It often happens that a student develops ideas while carving and fails because he cannot make up his mind, is afraid to commit himself, and continues to travel hopefully but never arrives. As the figure appears from the wood you may be depressed by the result, but if you persevere, you will find in time that the carving seems to take charge and you are working more by instinct and feeling than by intellect.

To return to the design of the carving. Apart from drawings and diagrams, you may find it very helpful to make a small model in clay, plasticine or plaster for guidance. For instance, if you intend to carve a figure 24 in. high, a model can be made 12 in., or even 6 in. high. This will help you form your idea and also help you to decide whether it is a good one. You can make a full-size plaster model which can be quite rough. In fact, this is often better as you should feel free to re-create the figure in wood. The model should be regarded as a pointer only and put aside fairly early and all attention should then be given to the carving itself.

You may find the early exercises I am going to suggest, such as an egg, completely uninteresting. However, as a carver you will discover that shape and form are enjoyable. I will not press this point as many readers will wish to make carvings with pictorial content. The most important consideration is that the carving should be enjoyable. Therefore carve a design that interests you.

CHAPTER SIX

Wood carving in practice

CARVING IN THE ROUND

First exercises

In learning to carve wood it is a very good plan to start with a few basic shapes. If you have been inspired to start carving by seeing some elaborate piece of ornament, put this out of your

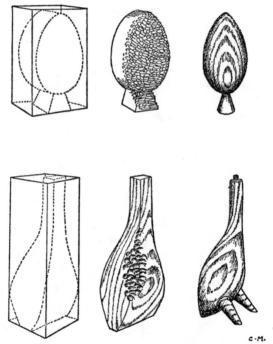

c·M.

Fig. 25. Simple exercises in the round.

mind for the time being. As a first exercise in the round attempt an egg as illustrated, or perhaps a cylinder, or cone. The actual carving of such shapes need not be a lengthy process, but in the course of making them you will learn some fundamental truths about wood and tools. You may prefer to carve an asymmetrical shape such as the lamp base (Fig. 25). This was a student's wood carving in ash and made from a block measuring 12½ in. × 4 in. × 4 in. Choose any shape that will enable you to carve broad surfaces. Do not start with a very small block of wood. The egg

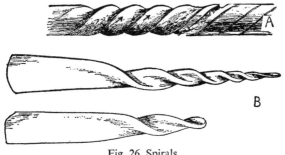

Fig. 26. Spirals.

form—large end uppermost—is recognized by the sculptor as a basis for the design of the human head, and if you manage to carve it you will be well on the way to carving a head in the round.

Whatever shape you choose, draw it clearly on the block of wood. Then saw off the unwanted corners, or roughly round the shape. The bow saw can be used for sawing curves. Secure the block to the bench by one of the methods described earlier. Commence cutting with a gouge of medium sweep or curve ½ in. to ¾ in. in size. Think of the sections of the form as you carve, working all over the shape; avoid making arbitrary holes in the surface. Keep to one gouge for some time. This will help you to carve consistently.

The spiral (see Fig. 26) is rather more difficult to carve, but is good practice in carving concave forms. For this exercise you should buy a 2 in. or 3 in. dowel from your local timber merchant. The drawing can be assisted by pinning a piece of string at the top of the dowel and winding it round spiral fashion. Draw a line along the string. Using a near flat gouge make a sharp cut on each side of the line at approximately 50 degrees and $\frac{1}{4}$ in. deep. Now cut a groove with a fluter or deep gouge in a central position

Fig. 27. Small carvings for mobiles.

between the lines. Work down from the first cuts to the center groove by means of a shallow gouge. This would be a good moment to practice hand-pushing the tool as described in Chapter 4, page 47. Spiral forms are fascinating to carve. The curves can be various or graduated, and the wood could be of asymmetrical shape. It is not always easy to visualize a form such as a spiral in the round and a model can be quickly made in plasticine and would be a useful guide (Fig. 26B).

Fig. 28. Carved toys by Yootha Rose.

I have advised a broad treatment for the beginner but you may be forced by circumstances to work small, or, on the other hand it may be your natural inclination. In this case toy-like carvings can be made from odd pieces of wood, dowels, old tool-handles etc. The Knight's Head (Fig. 27) was carved from the end of a hammer-handle, the legs and arms of the other figures are carved from dowels. Figure 29 shows a nursery mobile made from small

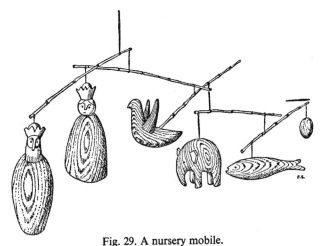

Fig. 29. A nursery mobile.

carvings. The arms of the mobile are made from cane, this is light and easy to drill. Strings, wires and split rings can be used for the attachments. The general pattern of the mobile will work well but you must adjust the design and balance to suit the weight of your carvings.

You should start making the mobile from the light end, that is where the fish appears in the diagram. If you use strong silk thread for the strings the objects will move freely. With wire the movement is more restricted and double rings at the junction with the cane will help. Some patience must be exercised but experimenting with mobiles is a fascinating occupation.

CARVING A BIRD

A bird has a fairly simple general shape and would be a good choice for your first carving in the round. The legs are the only part that present any practical difficulty. In the demonstration drawings the pigeon is in a roosting position so that this problem does not arise. Remember that the strength of the wood lies along the fibres of the grain. In our example the grain should go the length of the bird, that is from head to tail. You could try out a number of sketches yourself based on this idea. It will be comparatively easy for you to invent your own design. You probably see pigeons every day, or you may have a caged bird

Fig. 30. Design for a pigeon in the round.

to study. Remember when planning your design, that the carving must stand firmly on its base when finished. A base can be added or incorporated in the block. In the demonstration diagrams of the carving in progress you will see that the base is incorporated.

Draw a side view in the actual size of the carving (Fig. 30). With tracing paper make a second drawing of the same design. Now make another drawing of the bird as seen from above. This will give you an idea of the thickness of wood required. Allow one inch to spare in thickness, if you can, and a little extra length at the head and tail. This will leave room for modifications. Now cut out one of the side-view silhouettes, making it slightly larger all round. Lay this template or pattern on the block and draw round with chalk. Now screw the base of the block to a stout board, and cramp it to the bench. Alternatively, use the wood-carver's vise (Fig. 7).

Roughing out

Before you start carving with the gouge, a saw may be useful in two ways. First the obvious: by sawing off the corners (Figs.

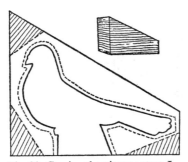

Fig. 31. Carving the pigeon: stage I.

31, 32), or round the shape, with a bow saw or bandsaw a certain amount of labor may be saved. The saw can also be used for cutting in toward the design and then splitting down in line with the grain (Fig. 35). This latter method must be used with great care so as not to saw too deeply and is not suitable for woods with a twisting or interlocking grain. Do not try to split the wood in lengths more than 3 in. at a time, as the grain may

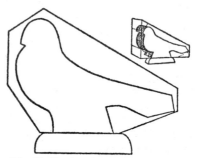

Fig. 32. Carving the pigeon: stage II.

change direction. Never try to split the wood without the saw-cut 'stop' which keeps the splitting under control. These stop-cuts can also be made with a sharp chisel when removing small pieces

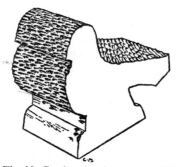

Fig. 33. Carving the pigeon: stage III.

of wood. Wood such as mahogany can split very easily at times and too much wood can be lost by a careless blow. When you have removed the corners and spare wood with the saw, put the

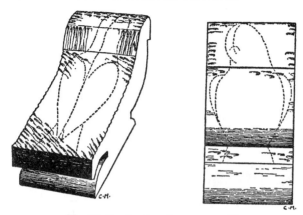

Fig. 34. Carving the pigeon: stage IV.

saw away as you will not need it again during carving. Now draw on the block again, making sure that you have planned the shape from the front and top (Fig. 34). If the block is wide enough you can give the head some movement.

Fig. 35. Carving the pigeon: stage V.

Fig. 36. Pigeon; carving in progress.

When you start with the mallet and gouge choose the latter in a medium size, ⅝ in. to ¾ in., and with a medium sweep. You must always be prepared to change the direction of your cut at the first sign of ragging or splitting, especially when faced by twisting grain or in the neighborhood of knots. In larger carvings it may be impossible to avoid all knots but by planning you can arrange that they are cut away, or in any case that they do not come in the center of a piece of detail. The very nature of carving in the round in wood will compel you to change cutting direction. This is quickly learned with practice and you will in the end cut in the right direction by instinct. It is quite safe to cut across the fibres

of the grain, but you will notice that when cutting with the grain
the wood has a polished appearance and if you are leaving a tool-
cut finish it is best to complete the carving in this way. If the cut
looks dull or ragged whichever way you cut, it is a sure indication
that your tools are blunt.

CARVING IN RELIEF

First exercises (Fig. 37)

As in carving in the round, a simple abstract form could be
the first exercise.

You will see that a pear-form is suggested, the various stages
being shown on one diagram. First draw the shape clearly on the
wood. The next process is known as 'setting in': in the diagram,
A marks the first groove cut round the drawing with a veiner,
fluter or pointing tool. At *B* a cut is made with a deep gouge.
C marks the cutting down round the shape with a near flat gouge.
D shows the background cut away with a gouge of medium sweep.
E is the full depth of the relief. *F* shows carving commencing with
a shallow gouge. At *G* some undercutting will give the illusion of
depth.

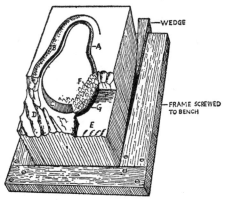

Fig. 37. Diagram showing seven stages in carving a relief.

All these processes should each be completed in turn round the whole pear form. The undercutting should be left till the last as you may wish to cut the form still deeper.

Potentialities of relief-carving

Even if you are a beginner, it is as well to be clear about the potential and the limiting factors in the carving of a relief. A relief is closer to the painted picture than work in three dimensions. The conception, at the outset, depends on drawing and although depth of carving can enrich and give the work a third dimension, a flat picture or pattern can be translated into a carving in relief. Thus the field of design for relief is very wide indeed. You have only to look at Indian relief carving in wood to realize that a lace-like delicacy can be achieved, or at the late German Gothic carvings in most museum collections in order to see that it is possible to carve a relief which is also three dimensional. The figures in these carvings are almost free from the background and attached to it so cunningly that they look as though they could step out of their frames. They may be joined to the background by the feet only, or at the back in one or two places. This type of 'tour de force' carving is not to all tastes. In the example (PLATE VI) of an Indian nineteenth-century carving you will notice that one of the elephant's legs and the trunk are completely free. The grain is running down the length of these parts, making them strong. From time to time stone has also been carved in this way, but stone does not have the fibrous strength of wood and these free parts are often damaged or completely knocked away.

You will see that it is possible to be really adventurous when carving relief in wood. You can also get this 'free' look in the design by deeply undercutting the figures or shapes yet leaving them attached to the background. It is not easy to do this in high relief without the help of the bent gouge. In high relief there is a greater play of light and shade and therefore greater legibility. This is obvious when you consider that a hole drilled in wood can appear black in contrast to the surface of the block. The drill is often used in carvings of both wood and stone. If you examine Indian, Greek or Roman carvings, the evidence of the drill is plain to see. It is often apparent in the curls of the hair, the eyes or in details of the drapery.

The background of a relief can be in flat areas that form part of the whole design, or the relief can be so enriched or crowded with figures that the background is not much in evidence. It is a mistake to think that the background must always be of uniform

Fig. 38. Design for a cockerel in relief.

depth from the face of the panel. It is better to concentrate on the subject matter and let the background look after itself. I would suggest that the beginner should not attempt a crowded design. Also, it is best to choose a single subject for the first carving: a head, an animal, or any shape that interests you. Cut the design fairly deeply. This will give you more scope. There are, however, plenty of fine examples of eighteenth-century English wood carving in very shallow relief. This is usually applied carving such as described later in this chapter, when in places the relief may not be more than $\frac{1}{8}$ in. thick. Such carving is difficult for an amateur with little experience in drawing. In a shallow carving the drawing is all-important. In a relief there is less margin for change and

modification. Therefore it is as well to spend time and thought on
the design and to take care with the drawing. If drawing is poor,
a very flat carving on a flat background can give the effect of
cut-outs in pastry. Such carving has a 'stuck on' appearance and
may well be very dull and uninteresting. The suggested design for
a cockerel in relief is simple but will also give scope for the use of
pattern and texture. It is intended as an example and even if you
decide to use the idea I would say that you should make some
changes and experiment. Do not be afraid to spoil a few pieces of
wood.

APPLIED DECORATION

Today for the most part furniture is plain and undecorated. In
modern furniture carved decoration is out of fashion. To stick
pieces of carved design arbitrarily on modern furniture is un-
thinkable for it has already been designed as a whole. A wide
revival of carving on mass produced furniture is unlikely.
However, if you have designed a piece of furniture there is no
reason why a certain amount of carving should not be incorporated. I would again stress that the piece should be conceived as
a whole and the carving appropriate to the object.

Architectural carvers, such as Mr H. Board (PLATE II), use
applied carving in the reproduction of period decoration of all
kinds, in restoration work, mantelpieces, mirrors and furniture.
An example shown (PLATE XVIII) is being carved in 1 in. pine. The
first requirement is a long back-board at least 1 in. thick. One or
two layers of paper are then stuck to the board with thin glue.
After the design has been made on paper, it is marked out on the
piece of wood to be carved either by the use of carbon-paper or
a template. Sometimes the design is made on thin detail-paper and
stuck to the wood. The general shape is then cut out by the fret-
saw and glued to the paper on the back-board. By this method
all the delicate parts of the design are supported and will not
break during the carving process. After the carving is finished,
it is separated from the back-board with the aid of a long knife.
This is slipped under the paper so cutting the carving free. The

ornament is now ready to be applied to its assigned place. PLATE XXI shows ornament applied to a copy of an eighteenth-century fireplace. The carved ornament is glued and pinned (Fig. 39). The pins used are the ordinary type used in sewing. The

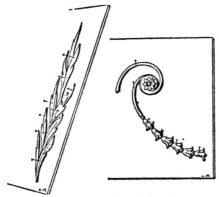

Fig. 39. Method of applying decoration.

heads of the pins are sunk and the holes filled. By using this method the finest decoration, only perhaps ¼ in. thick, can be carved by a skilled man without difficulty.

LETTER CUTTING IN WOOD

I must first stress that if you wish to cut letters in wood, some study of letters themselves is essential. The Roman letter holds a supreme place as a basis for the study of carved letters and you must spend time in drawing these before you start. When you have been carving letters for some time you need not slavishly follow the Roman forms. You will be able to make your own deviations, in fact design your own letters. It is only after a period of time that you will do this with success when you have come to appreciate the form and balance of the letters. All the problems of spacing and making satisfactory layouts of given inscriptions demand some experience. If you decide to carve the name of your house on the front gate with no previous study of the subject, the enlightened passer-by may well shudder at the sight. For anyone who has studied the subject, the ill-shaped letter is painful to see.

Excellent sheets of Roman lettering can be bought cheaply. There are also many books on the subject. Students and many young people think of letter cutting as boring. It is in fact an acquired taste. I know from experience that it can be enjoyable and very satisfying. In cutting letters you are dealing with form, proportion and abstract shapes. The fine laws evolved in Roman lettering are flexible and can be adapted to any given inscription.

Wood for letter cutting

It is wise to choose a close, even, and straight grained wood. Oak, quarter cut, is often used and is suitable for indoor and outdoor work. Lime wood is excellent but needs protection from the weather. The inscription should be worked out carefully on paper. When working on stone I usually draw on the tablet itself. With wood this is not advisable because the graphite of the pencil will get into the grain and the surface of the panel marked and damaged. It is best therefore either to use carbon-paper or to draw the letters on thin detail-paper and paste it on as seen in PLATE III where the late Mr A. G. Cole is carving an inscription in oak on a remembrance stand. Either of these two methods are sometimes used for stone also.

Cutting letters

For letter cutting you need very sharp fine bevelled chisels, gouges for curves, corner chisels for the serifs; parting chisels can also be used if the grain is very close or, as in wood engraving, on the end grain.

The letters can be carved in a number of ways. I personally prefer the incised V cut of approximately 60 degrees. A curved concave section can be used, or the letters can be raised. The latter method involves some labor in cutting down the background. It is better in this case to cut the letters with the edges very slightly sloping out, otherwise they will tend to look stuck on. The recessed curved letter looks well gilded and takes the light better than a V cut. If the inscription is in a poor light, gilding or painting will increase legibility.

CHAPTER SEVEN

Carving a life-size figure

I HOPE this chapter will prove useful to the young sculptor who has his first commission to carve a large figure in wood. The methods described will follow very closely those used in the 'The Risen Christ in Glory' (PLATES VII-XIII). It is likely that the setting for a large commission will be architectural. First the building or the plans for the building should be carefully studied. This can be the best stimulus in crystallizing the idea. If you are fortunate you may be working from the outset with the architect in a sympathetic spirit of co-operation, at the same time being given a free hand on the actual design of the figure. If you have confidence in your idea do not be too ready to compromise, this can spoil a good design.

If the building is a public one, a committee will want to see your drawings and sketch model for the figure. Some sculptors work only from drawings but I find the model indispensable in planning a large carving. It is advisable to spend a good deal of time and thought on the matter at this vital stage. Once the design is passed, you are to some extent committed. Make your idea as clear as possible, at the same time leaving room for modifications. The model is, of course, only the seed from which the work must grow and at no time should you think of slavishly following the sketch. On the other hand any vision and vitality in your first model must not be lost. These problems can only be solved by the artist following his own convictions.

There is, however, one point I would like to make. I have found that a student can design a figure on a small scale and on enlarging makes changes of which he is unaware. Therefore I would say that you should carefully appraise the sketch and try to see where its virtue lies. If it seems good, analyse the appearance of weight, size and movement you have achieved. Try not to lose this and only build from this foundation.

Some sculptors prefer to work from very rough sketches. I would make no rules about this. For my own part, in a commissioned work I like to solve the major problems at an early stage. It is a very different matter when carving for yourself. You may then prefer to carve direct, or with just a chalk drawing on the wood. The wood and joinery involved in a work on a large scale can be expensive and major changes in design can prove very costly. A drawing or painting of the carving in its setting is a great help in visualizing the whole aspect of the work in position. Another possibility and a help to the architect may be a photograph of your sketch model placed on the drawn elevation of the building. The photograph must be to scale, of course.

In making the sketch model, I would suggest a scale of 3 in. to 1 ft., that is ¼ scale. The sketch can be in clay, plaster, wax, or plasticine. As you will be using the sketch model while working, it is best to have it in a fairly permanent material. For instance, it would be best to cast the clay model and work from the plaster. Recently I have used plasticine for sketch models and found that it stands up to a good deal of handling. If you are designing a figure for a cross, make the cross also in order to have the whole design complete at the sketch stage.

When working out the cost of your carving, do not underestimate the materials. When the design has been passed, the wood can be ordered. We will take it, that the block is to be built up in 4 in. planks. The first move is to approach a reputable timber merchant who can supply good sound timber of the kind required. You may be able to visit the yard or shop in order to inspect the wood yourself. This is, in any case, most interesting and will help to increase your knowledge of the varieties of wood available and enable you to gain much general information of a useful kind.

A word about finance. You will want to pay for the wood soon after delivery. When the price for the carving has been agreed, it is quite usual to ask for a deposit fee in advance, in order to cover initial expenses.

The Christ figure is built up in 4 in. planks of lime wood. It is often called the sculptor's wood and I have found it excellent for this type of work. You must prepare templates of the pieces of timber required for building up the block. First make a set $\frac{1}{4}$ scale from your small model. Remember that you are designing a block that will contain the carving without cramping it in any way. Work with this aim in view. Simplify the line where you can and leave all subtleties of shape for carving. Do not arrange the pieces in such a way that butt-end or grain-end joints come across the figure. Where possible let the pieces run the whole length of the design. Joints will not be obtrusive when one piece of wood is glued on top of another. In fact, the block is literally 'built up' to the thickness required.

When you have made a template of each piece $\frac{1}{4}$ scale, enlarge these to full size. If the block is simple as in the case of the Christ figure, you can enlarge by calipers and a four-foot rule. Every 3 in. will equal one foot. You could also use the angle scale or squaring-up method described in Chapter 10. The templates can be made in thin card or strong paper. I use roofing felt for this purpose: it cuts easily but is strong and rolls up without tearing or cracking.

When you make the full-size templates, give yourself an inch or two to spare in every direction. You will buy the 4 in. planks of timber unplaned. After planing the thickness may be only $3\frac{1}{2}$ in. A carving needs more 'room' than a clay model. Although you must make your templates on the generous side, do not overdo it, and throw everything out of scale, by, for instance, making the figure 6 in. longer. Give yourself enough wood for some licence of movement, enough for some change of weight in the head, hands or feet. Form looks very different in a new material and certain changes are a legitimate translation from clay to wood.

Make at least three copies of your large templates. One for the timber merchant, one for the carpenter, and one for yourself. The timber merchant will not, as a rule, cut the shapes but he will need patterns in order to calculate the width and number of planks required. Ask the timber merchant for an estimate of the cost of wood in super-quality.

You must now find a carpenter. I think, on the whole, that it is best to approach a large firm because it will be better equipped to handle the job. The planing machine must be wide enough to take the wood. For instance, the Christ figure discussed in this chapter was approximately 14 in. across the chest without the arms, and small joinery firms are often only equipped with 12 in. machines. Also, the planks may be 10 ft. long and space will be needed for manipulation. The weight of these planks is considerable and three or four men will be needed to carry them. I have not so far had any difficulty in finding a firm ready to help with the cutting and carpentry. You should always remember, however, that this work may be out of their usual line of business and therefore you should be expeditious in all your dealings.

Having found a carpentry firm, arrange to have your planks delivered direct to their works for the wood to be cut and the block to be glued up. You should do the marking out on the planks yourself. Even if you have bought super-quality, there will be a few knots. By judicious marking out, these can be avoided or placed inconspicuously, and you will know where any blemishes are likely to be cut away in the process of carving. Arrange for the planks to be put on trestles. In this way you will be able to see both sides. Another important point is that the same kind of wood can vary in color. Lime, for instance, can vary from brownish pink to a very light yellowish pink. Therefore you should try to match up the color as well as you can in pieces that will lie adjacent to one another. Sometimes a marked color change is unavoidable and I have used bleach successfully to lighten the darker parts of lime wood. Bleach is not so successful on the dark and heavy woods such as rosewood and iroko. Lime, beech, ash and elm bleach easily. Oak, mahogany and walnut will bleach but need more than one application. Very good proprietary brands can be bought, and the best I have found is the two solution variety, obtainable only in one gallon quantities. All directions for use are supplied with the bleach. The drapery on the Christ figure was bleached to pure white with one application.

When you have examined the planks carefully for blemishes,

and color, lay on the templates. The grain must run the length of the long thin forms. As I have already explained in the section on the grain of wood, forms sawn across the fibres will be weak. When you are satisfied with the layout, draw round the templates with a stick of chalk. The planks are now ready for cutting. They will be carried to the bandsaw, one man guiding the plank while the others support the weight. Ask the machinist to cut the wood just outside your chalk line. The cutting is a quick process and will save you hours of work. When it is completed the cut pieces are fed through the planing machine. The wood is now ready for gluing and I would advise the sculptor to indicate clearly the position and order of the pieces. Mistakes can be made and what seems obvious to you may not be so to others. One of the new resin glues, used under pressure, will give you a joint on which you can rely. The seam will be virtually invisible from a short distance when carved.

Many sculptors are fearful of this method but if the job is really well done it is in my opinion the safest way to tackle a large carving. After all, wooden structures have for centuries been built in sections. The planks can also be dowelled to give extra strength, but in the case of good gluing woods carpenters are usually of the opinion that dowels are unnecessary. In the Christ figure dowels were used in the arms only.

Plan your studio space to receive the glued-up block. It will be an advantage if the ceiling is high enough for the figure to stand upright at some stage of the carving. A sloping position will be easier at first. It is a good idea to screw one or two 'stops' of 2 in. × 2 in. wood to the floor to prevent the block from sliding. Always take safety precautions when working on a large carving which, after all, may weigh five hundred pounds or more. This bulk is an asset in that cramps are superfluous, and the block will be steadied by its own weight. You will need a few strong boxes in order that you may raise and lower the figure as required. Every aid, such as step-ladders and mirrors, should be employed to get as many views of the figure as possible. You cannot hope to see the figure exactly as it will appear in its setting and if practicable a certain amount of carving can be done when the figure is in position.

When the block arrives, mark out the main features from your scale model. The rough shape is there already and this will be a great help in plotting depths and angles. In carving the Christ from the sketch model I did not use an enlarging scale, only a flexible rule, calipers and a 4 ft. straight edge. The quarter scale is very easy to work from by simple mental arithmetic. The sketch model, in fact, becomes less and less important as the larger work takes charge and if all goes well, it will be only used for an occasional reference. If the arms are free from the body, it is

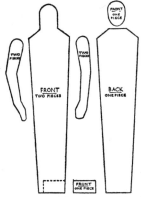

Fig. 40. 'The Risen Christ in Glory': templates for the figure.

possible to carve them separately, but they should be continually placed on the figure by a temporary dowel loose enough for the arm to be taken on and off with ease. In this way you can carve the arm in the bench vise getting at all parts such as the inner arm and the palm of the hand.

The choice of tools is important in carving a large work; 1 in. to 2 in. gouges can be used in roughing out. A large tool has more wood to push away and so more resistance is set up. A lignum vitae mallet weighing at least $2\frac{1}{2}$ lb. will save time and labor. As soon as your wrist has become accustomed to the mallet you will enjoy the way the sharp gouge and heavy mallet whip the spare wood away, and what seemed formidable is a delight after all. You will have to draw on the block from time to time. I find pencil illegible, and poster paint or chalk much better. Avoid inks or any other medium likely to stain the wood. I use white and raw umber powder color and this combination enables me to vary the drawing from light to dark at will. Lime wood soils very easily. This does not matter until the final stages when a protective coat of sealer or wax polish will keep the surface clean.

The fixing of the arms of the Christ figure is dealt with in the following chapter. The crown of this figure was very simple to make. A band of wood was carved on the head, and a band of copper screwed on. The copper rods were dropped into drilled holes round the top of the wooden band. It is difficult to drill the holes at exactly the right angle but this is simple to remedy, by dropping a metal tube over the rod—a piece of gas piping will do—and then pulling the copper rod to the correct angle. By this method the rod bends at the base only. The cross is made of Utile mahogany, 3 in. thick, and the 'shadow' of the crucifixion is in walnut veneer.

CHAPTER EIGHT

Adhesives and gluing

THE first evidence of the use of glue was found in an Egyptian tomb dated 1400 B.C. and there is little doubt that glue was used for some hundreds of years before this date. Pictorial evidence exists of Egyptian craftsmen boiling bones and hides to produce glue. In the Middle Ages the use of glue fell into a decline. The joints of furniture before A.D. 1500 were pegged and sometimes strengthened by iron straps. The first glue plant was founded at the beginning of the eighteenth century in Holland. Owing partly to the development of aircraft construction, the laminating of woods, and the growth of the plywood industry, animal glues have been improved and new adhesives evolved. Unless the carver is also engaged in furniture making or other wood constructional work, his use of glue is occasional. I do not, therefore, propose to write at length on the subject which is already covered in many excellent books on carpentry and woodwork.

Animal glues

The most famous of these, Scotch glue, made from the bones and skins of cows, is in substance similar to glue used by the Egyptians three thousand years ago, and has been in constant use in many countries for nearly three hundred years. It has great strength, is easy to prepare and is suitable for all interior work. Manufacturers do not advise the use of animal glues under tropical conditions.

Casein glue

This is made from milk and it takes 7,500 gallons to produce one ton of casein. It is produced in the Argentine, France, Poland, South Africa, and New Zealand. Casein glue is in white powder form and is mixed with cold water immediately before use. Chemically this is an alkaline glue and can cause brown staining on hardwoods. Casein glues are partly water and heat resistant but the joints need protection from the weather in exterior work.

Synthetic resins (accelerator-set)

These glues have a chemical setting action and must be used in conjunction with an accelerator or hardener catalyst. Synthetic resin glues are water and heat resistant.

Synthetic resin emulsions

These are strong and very easy to use. They have a quick action, are non-staining and are made to a number of different formulas to cover all types of work. These glues are not advised for use under humid and tropical conditions.

The gripping time of glues varies. If you are in any doubt about the length of time the joint should be cramped, leave it overnight; in the case of Scotch glue, twenty-four hours is not too long. As all the new glues are bought with full instructions for use, I will only describe the method of making Scotch glue.

Scotch glue

You will need a glue pot or double vessel. This can be improvised by using two tins, one that will stand inside the other, or a saucepan and a tin. The standard glue pot is a better proposition as it retains the heat well and will last a lifetime. You will also need a good quality 1 in. paint brush—soak it overnight before use. The glue is bought in slabs. Wrap one of these in a cloth or sacking and break it up into small pieces by hitting it with a hammer. The cloth prevents the pieces from flying about the room. Tip the glue into the inner vessel with just enough water to cover it. Put water in the outer vessel. Heat the pot, stirring the glue until it has melted to an even consistency. Do not let the water boil over into the glue. If the glue is watery, it is too thin; it should run off the brush like thin syrup. If it is too thick or lumpy, add a little hot water. Remove any scum on the surface.

Scotch glue must be used hot. It is therefore necessary to work quickly. Apply the glue liberally to the wood surface and cramp without delay.

Glued joints

A glued joint, well made, is not weak or unsightly. It is often stronger than the wood itself. If you have ever dismantled mahogany furniture, you may have noticed that the wood sometimes breaks but leaves the joint intact. Many of Grinling Gibbons' carvings are made up of $2\frac{1}{2}$ in. planks of lime wood, glued together. (See Fig. 18, p. 51.)

Pressure must be applied to joints at the time of gluing, either by the vise cramps or by machine press. It is most important that the surfaces to be glued should be clean. Also that they should be flat and true. If you cannot use a plane, find a carpenter who will do this part of the operation for you. A slightly convex surface will give an open joint. Sometimes the surface is planed or shot very slightly concave in the center, in order to give a good joint at the edges. In this case the cramps are placed in the middle of the wood. The surfaces can also be scored by an old saw or the edge of a rasp, to give an extra bite for the glue. You can test the flatness of a surface with the aid of a metal straight edge or by holding the edge of your plane across the surface. Arrange to have the window or light behind the edge; it is then quite easy to see whether the surface is true. Swing the edge at different angles on the surface in order to check every part. Planing a true surface is not easy for the amateur and needs practice. Should the carver wish to prepare the wood himself, I do advise that he get general woodwork instruction either from the many books on the subject or at a class in carpentry.

Rubbed joints

A rub-joint can be very satisfactory if the wood is small enough to hold in the hand. Fix one piece in the vise with the surface to be glued uppermost, apply the glue to both pieces of wood. Press the second piece of wood hard on the piece in the vise, rubbing at the same time to expel the air and surplus glue. In a few seconds the wood holds firm and the joint is made.

Spring dogs

The spring dog (Fig. 41) is very useful when gluing up delicate work or for repairs. It can be made from the type of upholstery spring illustrated.

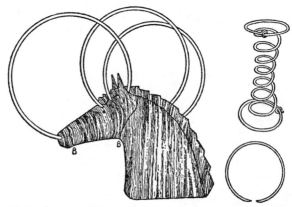

Fig. 41. Spring dogs. *Left:* used in gluing up delicate carving, points marked B indicate breaks. *Top right:* upholstery spring can be cut and used for this purpose. *Bottom right:* example of a spring dog.

Dowelled joints

When the carver wishes to join a limb to the body, a strong jointing method must be adopted. The mortise-and-tenon, or the dovetail, are both good methods but not advisable unless you have some skill in general woodwork. The dowelled or pegged joint, however, can be easily mastered by the amateur. It is frequently used by carvers in all sorts of ways.

When making a dowelled joint, the dowels must be of the same diameter as the holes. A brace and bit is used for drilling. If the dowel is driven in from the outside of the carving (Fig. 42, I), the operation is very simple but the dowel end will show and this is not always desirable on small work. The other method is to use the dowel on the inside of the joint (Fig. 42 II). Make sure that the holes are deep enough to take the dowel at the same time avoiding a large gap at the end. You can gauge the depth by putting an elastic band round the bit at the length required. Make a saw cut down the length of the dowel (Fig. 42 IV)

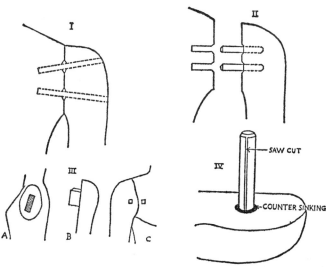

Fig. 42. Dowelled joints. I. Fixing an arm at the shoulder with dowels driven in from the outside of the figure. II. Interior dowelled joint. III. Egyptian method for fixing arms of wood figures: A and B mortise-and-tenon. C. The tenon pegged.

to take the surplus glue, otherwise too much surplus glue may prevent the joint from closing. Make sure that the holes in both pieces to be joined are in alignment. This latter problem varies with each carving. If the sides of the joint are straight, measurements can be taken. But if the shape is free, as in the case of an arm and shoulder, a template of the joint section with hole centers marked will be found very useful. I have used a wood

90   WOOD CARVING

template with the holes drilled in the appropriate places. The thickness of the template acts as a guide and allows the holes to be drilled in perfect alignment.

The easier method of drilling right through from the outside was used in the Risen Christ (Fig. 43). In a large work of this kind the dowels are hardly visible, especially if the color is well matched. The arms in this figure are heavy and free from the body so that a strong joint was necessary. Three $\frac{1}{2}$ in. dowels were used

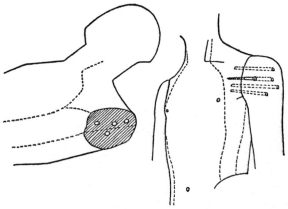

Fig. 43. Dowelled and screwed joint.

on each side and a $4\frac{1}{2}$ in. screw. The screw was used to draw the joint tight before the dowels were driven in. Cramping is not easy on a work of this size but sash cramps can be used for large work as shown in figure 10.

Jointing methods used by the Egyptians

The Egyptians used jointing methods for figures in both wood and stone. For wood the mortise-and-tenon joint was in common use. The tenon was fixed by wooden pegs as shown in figure 42, III. Their wooden statues were covered with gesso and painted.

CHAPTER NINE

Texture, finish and color

FINISH should be a natural outcome of your efforts to complete the form of the carving as well as you can. When you are satisfied with the look and shape of your work it is time to stop. If you favor a tool-cut texture, do not finish by imposing a uniform tooled texture all over the surface. This can be very monotonous and mechanical in appearance. Rather let the surface treatment come about by the process of carving the shapes. Surface glitter, whether it be varnish or superficial texture, will add nothing to the real value of your work. It is a mistake to be over-anxious to arrive at the finished product. When you start carving you are to some extent groping your way along the road to some achievement. In almost every case this does not come easily. As you carve you will discover the texture, color, and grain of the wood you are carving. If the grain is strong, a smooth finish will give you the maximum grain figure. This can be an inspiration in itself. On

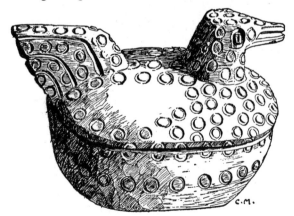

Fig. 44. African box.

the other hand, it may act as a camouflage and obscure some form you wish to make clear. Then, perhaps, a tool-cut surface is more appropriate.

The natural color is an important feature of wood and should be considered before you start the carving. The color of a block of wood, especially if air seasoned, can be deceptive from the outside. For instance, sycamore can look a silver grey on the surface but is pure white when cut. Teak can also look a dirty grey before cutting and its true rich brown becomes apparent only when you start to carve. A very dark wood, such as ebony, can give pleasure when highly polished, but on the other hand, form tends to get 'lost' in the very blackness of the wood. Steam affects the color of some woods. It is used by timber merchants to spread the color more evenly, as in the case of walnut, and to turn beech pink. Many woods tend to change color and are darkened by the passage of time. Lime will turn from near white to warm pink in a matter of a few weeks so that a part of your carving worked at an earlier date may show a definite color change. However, it will all settle down to the same color after the carving is completed.

You may wish to paint or gild parts of a carving. Gesso has been used as a ground for painting on wood for literally thousands of years, the best known early examples being the Egyptian wooden statues. Gesso is also an excellent ground for gilding. It will, of course, cover grain but also all flaws and joints. It is used to achieve a silky smooth finish. In the nineteenth-century English Noah's Ark animals were gessoed and painted. Examples of these toys can be seen among the toy collections of various museums and galleries.

Gesso

This can be made with plaster of Paris or whiting and size. Size can be made from gelatine. The plaster of Paris should be of fine quality and slaked by keeping it covered with water for at least four weeks, renewing the water each day. Whiting can be bought ready for use but the plaster of Paris gesso is considered to be the best. For gelatine size 1 oz. of commercial or edible gelatine should be added to 16 oz. of water. Melt the gelatine in the water by means of a double saucepan, but do not allow it to boil. Now let the size cool for testing: firm to the touch, the size is of the right consistency. Heat up the size again until melted. If you have used the 16 oz. quantity of water, stir in 24 oz. of whiting or plaster of Paris. If the latter is of very fine quality, you may need a little less than 24 oz. When made, the gesso should be of a thin creamy texture, flowing easily from the brush.

Applying gesso to wood. The wood should be clean and free from polish of any kind. First apply a coat of size and allow to dry for at least twenty-four hours. If the wood is very porous, a second coat can be applied. Rub down lightly with sandpaper when perfectly dry. Brush on the first coat of gesso. You can rub this in with the fingers to make sure of a good grip. When the coat dulls, that would be in approximately fifteen minutes, apply another coat. Never let the gesso dry between each application. Three coats should be sufficient. Rub down again with fine sandpaper when it is perfectly dry. A final coat of thin size will finish the job and the work is now ready for painting or gilding.

Painting on gesso. Tempera painting on gesso has a fine brilliance. Good quality powder color is mixed with yolk of egg. A little water can be added. If this method is used on toys, the painting should be sealed by a coat of spirit varnish. Oil paint can be used on gesso; it is advisable, however, to apply a thin undercoat of flat oil paint before the finishing coat.

Gilding on raw wood

Fine gilding and burnishing is a trade in itself and does not come within the scope of this book. The carver may occasionally wish to use a little gold and the transfer gold is not too difficult for the amateur to manage. If you are gilding raw wood, first seal it with a number of applications of white of egg and water. This mixture is known as 'Glair'. I use three whites to one pint of water. On mahogany I found that four coats were necessary.

Each coat must be allowed to dry before the next is applied. There will be a slight sheen on the wood when it is ready for gilding. The French slow gold size is advisable for most work. This size is applied and left for fifteen hours. If the weather is cold and damp, you may have to wait longer before gilding. If the size shows wet on the transfer paper, more time must be given. You will be able to continue gilding up to twenty-four hours and in damp weather conditions this time can often be extended.

Wax polishing

There are many ways of finishing the surface of wood, but for wood carvings wax polishing is the best. It has little effect on the color of the wood apart from making it slightly richer in tone. It produces a soft shine, pleasant to the eye and touch. Beeswax is the best basis for hand-applied polish. Other waxes can be added to it but this will be discussed later. Varnish and cellulose lacquers give a much higher gloss but this will not improve your carving, it will only cheapen its appearance. There are, however, a few disadvantages associated with wax polishing. These can be overcome if a little care is taken. I will deal with these difficulties first.

Wax by itself does not seal the grain of wood as effectively as shellac, varnish or lacquer. Dirt can therefore penetrate more easily. Wax tends to 'sink' into the softer parts of the wood, or into end grain. This 'sinking' makes the polish uneven and dull in places. This applies chiefly to the softer woods and with these, therefore, it is advisable to use a sealer before wax polishing. White french polish is a very effective sealer and is easy to use. If you buy this polish ready made up, buy also the solvent which is methylated spirit, for thinning down. Two thin coats of sealer should be sufficient. Apply the polish quickly with an inch paint brush, rubbing well in. Do not get the brush too full of polish and avoid runs. Allow the first coat to dry thoroughly. On soft wood you will find that this first coat raises the grain slightly. Rub the carving over very lightly with 0 grade sandpaper. Now apply the second coat and allow it to dry. The carving is now ready for wax polishing. The hard, heavy woods can be finished with wax polish alone but a sealer can be used in places such as end grain if the wax tends to sink.

Making a beeswax polish. Although furniture polish can be used on your carving, it is a very simple matter to make a high quality one yourself. Beeswax can be obtained in a bleached form. This is light yellow in color and is best for such woods as pine, sycamore and lime. Raw beeswax is brown and can be used on the darker woods. To make a small quantity of polish shred 3 oz. of beeswax—a coarse cheese grater can be used for this purpose. Place the beeswax in a small saucepan and just cover with turpentine or turps substitute. Now half fill a larger saucepan with water and heat on a low flame. Place the smaller saucepan containing the beeswax and turpentine in the saucepan of hot water. The water jacket is essential as the polish ingredients are very inflammable. Stir gently until the wax is dissolved, then allow it to cool. It will set in a paste-like form easy to use. If the polish is too liquid, add more wax and heat up again; if it is too stiff add more turpentine. You now have an excellent polish but variations can be made by adding other waxes. Carnauba wax can be added to beeswax, but only up to fifty per cent of the beeswax quantity. Carnauba is a very hard wax which is difficult to apply unless used with softer types. Candelilla wax is similar and rather less expensive. Paraffin wax is cheap and soft but this should be used in only small proportions, never more than one-third to two-thirds of harder wax. A soft wax marks easily and picks up dirt. Rosin may also be used to give a harder finish in a dark polish. It is as well to melt this first and then to add it gradually to the mixture. A clothes brush, shoe brush or rag can be used to apply the polish. A hog-hair paint brush is useful to get the wax into awkward corners. Rub the wax well in, then leave it alone for a day because the turpentine must have time to evaporate before your true wax surface is achieved. Then polish it with a clean rag. Linen rags are excellent for this purpose but, in any case, avoid a material that is soft or fluffy.

CHAPTER TEN

Enlarging and reducing scales

I DO not, as a rule, attempt to enlarge with exact accuracy from a small sketch. I prefer to have some licence to modify the design. However, at times scales for enlarging and reducing can be very useful, particularly if the beginner wishes to copy some given design. Students often use reducing scales when working from the live model. You should try to train your eye and not to resort to scales and measurements unless really necessary. If your drawing is weak, it is possible to work with a few guiding measurements and then to try and use your eyes and judgement. Temperaments vary in these matters and some will enjoy making very accurate and meticulous copies. This, however, can be paralysing to creative thought and design.

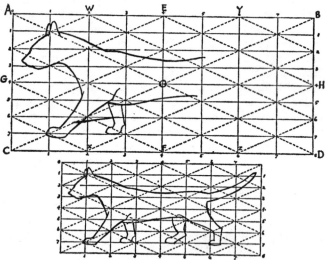

Fig. 45. Enlarging a design for relief by squaring up.

I describe in this chapter a few simple methods of enlarging
and reducing by linear measurement, using the squaring-up
method and angle scales. A number of other methods, such as
the pointing machine, the pantograph, the three-caliper-and-post
method, proportional dividers, and the wooden-frame method,
will be found in publications on the methods of sculptors.

Enlarging a design for relief by squaring-up

This is a very old method which can be used for enlarging or
reducing. Examine the diagram of the cat design (Fig. 45). Draw
a rectangle to the required size. This should be in the same proportion in length and breadth as the small design. First draw the
diagonals from *A* to *D*, and then from *B* to *C*. This will give you
the center *O*. Draw lines *EF* and *GH*. Again draw the diagonals

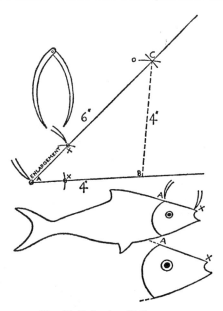

Fig. 46. Enlarging 1½ times.

EH, FH, GE, and *GF*. This will give you the position of the vertical lines *WX* and *YZ*. Continue this process until the units
are small enough to give accuracy in drawing. Now number
the vertical and horizontal lines. By noting carefully where the
drawing crosses the line pattern you will be able to enlarge the
design with ease.

Enlarging by using the angle scale

The angle scale for both enlarging and reducing is very simple
to use as soon as the principle is understood. Figure 46 shows a
diagram showing the enlargement of a fish design to 1½ times. In
this scale any two measurements can be used for making the angle,
providing that the ratio is the same: for instance, 4 in. and 6 in.,
6 in. and 9 in., or 9 in. and 13½ in. If you take the first two
measurements suggested, proceed as follows:

Enlarging 1½ times. Draw a line *AB*, 4 in. in length. Set the
calipers or pencil compasses at 4 in. and from point *B* describe arc
O. Set the calipers at 6 in. and from point *A* describe an arc inter-

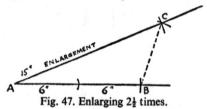

Fig. 47. Enlarging 2½ times.

secting arc *O* at point *C*. Draw line *AC*. Any given measurement
on the small design, as for instance *AX* on the fish's head, should
be taken along the line *AB* once only, then up from *X* to intersect
line *AC* at point *X*. From this point of intersection down to *A*
is the 1½ enlargement.

Enlarging to 2½ times. Make the angle as shown in the illustra-
tion for this scale. The only difference from the 1½ scale is that
in this case you must measure twice along *AB* before intersecting
AC in making the angle, and in every subsequent measurement
to be enlarged.

If the enlargement is to be over 3 times you must then measure 3 times on line *AB*.

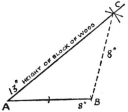

Fig. 48. Enlarging scales for odd sized blocks of wood.

Enlarging scales for odd sized blocks. If you have an odd sized block of wood, say, 13 in. high, and you wish to work from a model 8 in. high, you can make an open scale as shown in figure 48. Proceed to take measurements as in the scale for 1½ times

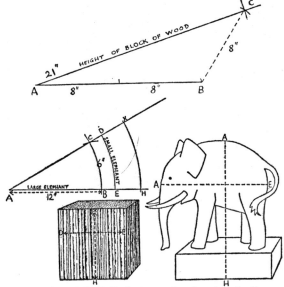

Figs. 49 & 50. Reducing scales: ½ scale reduction.

enlargement. Again I would mention that if the block is over twice the height of your model, it will be necessary to measure twice along the line *AB* before intersecting *AC* (Fig. 49).

Half scale reduction. The angle reducing scale is very simple to make and easy to use. In the case of the elephant (Fig. 50) all measurements are to be reduced by half for carving the animal half size. To make this scale, draw the line *AB* 12 in. in length. With the calipers at 12 in. on point *A* describe an arc from *B*. Set the calipers at 6 in. and from *B* describe another arc to cross the first at *C*. Make the angle by drawing a line from *A* to *C*. Any measurement, as for instance *A* to *H* on the large elephant, is taken by the calipers and an arc described from *A* across the angle: in this measurement it is the arc *XH*, and gives the height of the elephant and base in the small block.

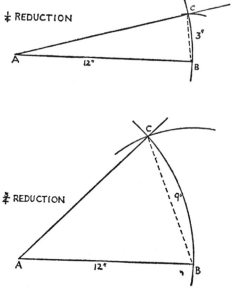

Fig. 51. Reducing scales: ¼ reduction and ¾ reduction.

This scale can be used in any size of reduction. Other examples given here are for $\frac{1}{2}$ and $\frac{3}{4}$ reductions. Providing *AB* and *BC* are at the ratios you require, the measurements are arbitrary. For example, you can use the height of the model to be reduced as the long measurement, and the height of the small block of wood as the short measurement. By using the angle scale so produced, it is simple to test the block for other dimensions. In this way you can find out whether the block is a suitable shape for the figure you wish to reduce. If the figure and block are both too large for measurement by the calipers, divide both lengths by a half or quarter. For example, in the case of a figure of 4 ft. 4 in. in height and a block of 3 ft. you can make the angle by using the length 1 ft. 1 in. and 9 in., a quarter division of both measurements.

The plumb-bob, square and set-square can be used as aids for measurements in depth. The caliper points can also be crossed for taking interior measurements (Fig. 52).

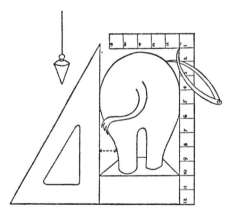

Fig. 52. Further aids to measurements in depth.

CHAPTER ELEVEN

Attitudes to wood carving

I. THE SCULPTOR AND THE SPECIALIST

FOR the sculptor wood is only one of the media in which he works. Stone, clay, cement, plaster, wax, metals, and in recent years plastics, are some of the diverse materials that come under his hand. He is likely to have a bias towards certain media, a liking for one or the other. During some periods he will prefer one medium, or circumstances may alter his course of work. To make a living as a sculptor he will often have to be ready to tackle any material. This is not necessarily a bad thing as it widens his powers and experience. He would be a superman if he knew all the answers to all questions involved in the use of every tool and all materials in such a wide field. He is gathering knowledge all the time but never knows it all. He may not do more than one wood carving a year but because of his natural aptitude for design and appreciation of form he can produce sculpture in wood.

The wood carver specialist, on the other hand, carves wood all day and every day, and is usually quite an expert at carpentry. He may be attached to a firm of wood carvers or run such a workshop himself. His skill is admirable. He can carve the most complicated ornament with sureness and dexterity. In the speed of carving ornament he can make rings round many sculptors. He is chiefly concerned with traditional wood carving design and is engaged in copying and restoration work. He does not make his living by creating new works of art but by repeating forms already established. From the aesthetic point of view it can be argued that there is an over-emphasis on craftsmanship to the detriment of creative work, and the cleavage between such craftsmen and sculptors may be great, and not easily bridged. We can look back to a time in Europe in the fifteenth century when the wood carver was carpenter, designer and creative artist in one, an ideal state of affairs. There is perhaps little profit in looking back and if we then look at things as they are now in America, we can say there are pockets where traditional wood carving is pursued and native skill and craftsmanship flourishes.

Harold Board's workshop is typical, and an example of the fine decorations and carvings produced is illustrated in PLATE XXI. Carvers such as David Pye work as individuals, producing beautiful objects that fit into the twentieth-century scheme of decoration (see Appendix B). Sculptors such as Alan Durst have stimulated many younger artists into using wood as a medium for sculpture. Established sculptors like Ossip Zadkine, Henry Moore, F. E. MacWilliam, Willi Soukop and Elizabeth Spurr, use wood as one of their media. It is unlikely that the use of wood will ever die out. No other material can exactly take its place and it will, I think, forever play a part in our surroundings, whether it be for building, furniture or sculpture.

II. The Human Figure

From earliest times the human anatomy has been studied and used by the artist. Canons of proportion have been worked out by the Egyptians and the Greeks. The study of the living and the dead in humans and animals has been part of the artist's experience for many centuries. This interest waxed and waned. The great artists of the Renaissance such as Leonardo da Vinci dissected the human body in a spirit of scientific discovery. Dissection would certainly be repugnant to most artists today. Perhaps the spirit of inquiry is less intense. George Stubbs (1724–1806), the great English painter was the last artist anatomist to undertake exhaustive research in this field. The study of the living model is still a valuable part of the student's training today. This and the study of works of art is the food his creative power needs in order to grow.

The beginner who wishes to carve figures would certainly profit by some drawing from the model. If it is not possible to attend classes, he should draw his family and friends. An anatomy book is of little use unless allied to observation of people. In books you will find the average proportions of men, women and children. This does not mean that your aim should be to carve the average man. To work with the latter concept in mind is likely to produce the dullest work. We can say that knowledge and interest in structure is valuable but that all such knowledge must be re-created by the artist.

In the stone figures on Chartres Cathedral in France we see

Fig. 53a. *Idol*, wood of the bread-fruit tree, Caroline Islands.

Fig. 53b. *House post*, Solomon Islands.

elongation of the figure, the head enlarged and the shoulders narrow. Here we have a superb example of sculpture and architecture perfectly related. On the same cathedral we can see smaller figures with large heads and short bodies, as in the carving of Aristotle. A figure can be given giant proportions by making the head, hands and feet small in relation to the body. It follows, therefore, that proportion is a matter of choice for the artist and that scale is affected by the relative size of parts of the body.

If we remember that changes and modifications have always been employed by artists, modern deviations from 'natural' proportion cease to startle or surprise. The work of children, primitives and amateurs fall into quite another category, for their work is not based on any profound knowledge of the human figure. The child and the primitive have innocence on their side, but the amateur in our civilized society is bombarded by visual impressions of the worst kind in mass produced knick-knacks and many other vulgarities. Therefore he must learn to select influences by the process of recognizing real creative ideas and qualities. These can always be found, but the habit of looking for them must be acquired.

The human head

The layman, looking at figure sculpture, invariably gives most attention to the rendering of the head. In modern sculpture the head is often simplified and expression given by movement and shape rather than facial expression. In such works as the Madonna illustrated in figure 54, we can see a fine basic shape with attention also given to the carving of the features. If the beginner wishes to carve the features on a head, he should leave them uncarved in any detail until the whole head-form is established. It is a help, perhaps, to remember that it is possible to recognize a person at a distance purely by shape, balance, and character of movement— to consider the poise of the head on the neck and shoulders, and the relative weight of skull to detail will be a productive approach. The back is no less important than the front and the aim of the carver should be to visualize the head as one complete unit.

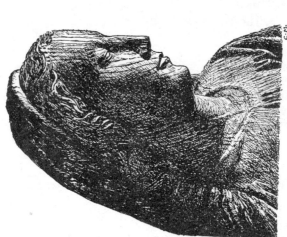

Fig. 54. Detail of *Madonna* in wood, Oldenburg, Germany, 1460.

III. Freedom in Design

The professional artist, if working for himself, is quite free to paint, carve or design as he feels inclined. His mind is full of things seen, liked or disliked. He may be preoccupied with the past, the present or the future, or all three, but for him design is of supreme importance. On the other hand, the amateur who just wants to carve a few things in his spare time may not consider his problems in the field of design in any way complex. Nevertheless, as soon as he makes something with his hands he has joined the stream of art activity for good or ill. If you are such a one there can be no harm in thinking about design for five minutes, but thinking about it for five years is better. I must point out that once a man starts to appreciate the shape and design of objects around him he finds it quite impossible to stop doing so.

The carver, therefore, free to make any form or shape he pleases, is in a position of power. He need not be bound by rules and regulations. He must, however, realize that as in living we are assailed by trash, vulgarity and insincerity, so in art can such vices distort the vision. 'Ugliness' and 'Beauty', 'Good' and 'Bad' in art have always been a matter for argument among artists and critics. If, therefore, you are making your first design for carving, do not start with the idea that you know all the answers as to what is good and what is bad in art. A casual acquaintance with design is not a basis on which to form final opinions. Start in a modest way with an open mind.

Fig. 55. *Crocodile,* Central Solomon Islands.

To the professional artist, designing is a serious business, but I do not overlook the fact that to the amateur it may be a light-hearted recreation. Design can have many ingredients including humor, charm and humanity. The carved mask of a primitive society may be frightening, comic, or grotesque. It can still, however, be a fine design. The vitality may spring from deep religious or social significance, a real belief in the power of the mask to scare away the demon. We may have no driving force of this kind, but if something good is to result, some excitement, some feeling and enjoyment of carving must be present. Your work is an extension of yourself and speaks plainly to the eye of the understanding spectator. It will always have your own personal stamp. Two portraits of the same person by different artists are never alike and yet both can be good portraits.

It may be that your first effort will only proclaim your ineptitude, but do not worry too much. If you feel the basic idea is good, then try again. Remember that a good idea inexpertly carved is better than a bad idea beautifully carved. In fact, slickness of technique can make a poor design even more unpleasant to look upon. It is possible for a man to enjoy the process of carving and copying with little or no thought about the quality of his design. He may put technique above all and will disregard any work, whatever its merits if in his opinion, it is not well carved. This is to live in a blind alley without the light of ideas and warm vitality. A trade carver who is working for his living as a carver may have no choice in the matter. However, having mastered the technique of carving he can make his own experiments in his spare time.

At the other extreme is the young artist who affects to despise technical achievement, who bristles at the idea of finish and is preoccupied with the excitement of texture and temporary effects. He will make objects of driftwood, rusty iron, silver paper and anything that comes to hand. Experiment is natural and healthy. These movements in art today are strong and cannot be ignored. Giants such as Picasso can make a picture out of bric-à-brac, but they are also masters of the more conventional techniques.

For my own part I think that art at its best will keep its roots in organic form and that the human element in the sculptor's work has a permanent place. An exclusive diet of abstract art is unsatisfying. Without doubt one can enjoy the quality in material such as wood, bronze and stone, of polish, patina and texture. All these things can play an important part in the final completion of a work of art.

Words such as 'Beauty' and 'Craftsmanship' are bitter on the tongue of many students today. Perhaps in the age of nuclear weapons the young artist does not feel that his work can have a permanent existence. Power, speed and excitement play their part. Horrors and war can fascinate those who have not experienced either. This aspect of art may disturb older generations but the trends cannot be forcibly changed, even if this were desirable, which is open to doubt. Art is always a manifestation of life and the age in which we live.

CHAPTER TWELVE

Historical background

by PEGGY MILLS

WOOD is a perishable material and has not the same continuous history as stone. Ancient stone carvings are still unearthed; Greek bronzes are still being fished out of the sea. But wood will not survive neglect and must be specially cared for if it is to endure. There are many gaps—many civilizations which have no wood carvings to represent them.

The earliest sculptures that still exist are of bone and baked clay, stone and bronze, but there can be no doubt that prehistoric man carved wood—even if only for his axe-handles. He lived in the forests; fallen trees would be more plentiful than suitable pieces of stone.

EGYPT

But wood can only survive in favorable conditions, and so far as is yet known, Egypt is the only country where these have existed. Eleven wooden relief panels were found there in 1860, having been preserved by the drifting sands for over four thousand years, and they are believed to be the oldest in the world. They were discovered in the tomb of Pharaoh Hesy-Ra at Sakkara, and each measures about two feet by one foot six inches. The figure of the Pharaoh (Fig. 56) is portrayed in the typical Egyptian pose, finely drawn and sensitively carved.

The Egyptians went on using child-like conventions long after they could have dispensed with them. Egyptian art being entirely religious, the conviction was that all art-forms, like all the rites and ceremonies, had been laid down by the gods in ancient times, and could never be altered. There is nothing peculiarly Egyptian about this; right down to the present day, many religions have maintained a strict conservatism in form and ceremony.

The earliest three-dimensional wooden figures yet discovered date from 2500 B.C. Three were found at Sakkara, and the most famous of them was nicknamed Sheik-el-Beled by the native workmen who dug it up, because it reminded them of their

Fig. 56. Egyptian wood panel, 2950 B.C., *Pharaoh Hesy-Ra* at Sakkara.

village-mayor. The carving is about 3 ft. high and is, again, in a conventional Egyptian pose: striding forward with the weight on both feet and carrying a staff. The eyes are inlaid, and the lifelike vitality of the head is almost startling. The carving technique, like that of the relief panel, shows perfect confidence and control.

Realistic portrait-heads for the statues were at all times

considered essential. The sculptor was required to carve an 'imitation man' to be inhabited by the soul after death.

Wood was scarce in Egypt, and the acacia and sycamore, the only trees growing there suitable for carving, were so precious as to be considered sacred. In countries where there are forests, wood is sometimes used as a cheaper substitute for rare and precious materials. Egypt had a different scale of values, judging by an observation in a letter from a minor king to a Pharaoh in 2000 B.C. 'In your country, gold is as common as dust . . .' Wood was used for royal statues as well as for less important figures, such as courtiers, officials, priests, scribes and architects. Relief panels were always in wood or limestone.

The wood carvings were placed in the elaborate tombs, where, it was believed, the Pharaoh would live on, so long as his embalmed body lay there undisturbed. He was surrounded by all the things he would need to take with him into the next life, and his servants were represented by little figures engaged in all kinds of farm and domestic work. Many of these are in wood, and some of the most remarkable are of women with long narrow figures and long skirts, walking upright and carrying baskets of offerings on their heads.

Wood was used for many purposes besides statues: for thrones, coffins and furniture of all kinds, and for the inner cores of metal statues. A figure was carved in wood and then covered with thin sheets of gold, copper or bronze, hammered on to its shape and fastened with nails. Every nation has found its way toward the craft of hollow casting in bronze by first using the wooden-core method.

So much wood was needed, that a regular sea-borne trade was started with Syria and the Lebanon, importing cedar, cypress, juniper, pine and yew, while ebony was brought from the Sudan.

After lasting almost continuously for over two thousand years, Egypt's power began to decline in about 1000 B.C., and was finally broken by a series of foreign conquests. But, although the long tradition of art also declined, nothing could subdue the strong, characteristic style of the Egyptians, and it was adopted by each conquering nation in turn—even the Greeks and the Romans. Only in A.D. 638 with the Arab conquest did the art of Egypt finally come to an end.

MESOPOTAMIA

The early history of Mesopotamia, the land between the Tigris and the Euphrates, is not so well known as that of Egypt: nor has the country been so thoroughly excavated. But its civilization, art and culture were equally great, and may be even more ancient. They were rival powers, but they evidently had little contact except in battle, and did not influence each other.

The sculpture that has come down to us from the three successive civilizations of Mesopotamia—Sumerian, Babylonian and Assyrian—has nothing in common with the Egyptian. A great many beautiful small pieces have been found but there are very few large-scale figures in the round. A great variety of materials were used, but hardly any wood carvings are even known to have existed. Mesopotamia has few trees, and terracotta was widely used for every purpose—even the building-material being of sun-baked bricks.

Although the brick-built temples were more susceptible to destruction than the Egyptian stone buildings, Mesopotamian culture has never really died out. Not only their achievements in the early forms of science and philosophy, but their decorative arts were inherited by the Persians and were passed on through the Greeks and later through the Moslems to Europe. The Persian genius for lyrical design, seen in their pottery, textiles and carpets originally stemmed from the ancient Sumerians.

THE ORIENT

In the ancient civilizations of China and India, wood carving is a craft of great antiquity, and in all countries of the Far East—Japan, Burma, Siam, Java, Indonesia—wood has always been used extensively for building, both interior and exterior. Sculptures of the Orient, however, are a study in themselves, and are outside the Western line of tradition which is the subject of this chapter.

GREECE

No Greek wood carving has survived, but there is evidence in the writings of Pausanias, a Roman who travelled in Greece during the second century A.D., that there were hundreds of wooden statues of gods and athletes still standing there in his time. According to his descriptions, some were very simple, like huge pillars, with heads and hands carved on them; some figures were dressed in real draperies. A number of them were already very ancient, and were held in great veneration by the Greeks. The woods known to have been used were: cedar, cypress, myrtle, oak, laurel, apple, pear, olive and ebony.

There can be little doubt that the wood carvings were like the Archaic figures in marble that have come down to us from the seventh and sixth centuries B.C. These were evidently based on the Egyptian striding figure, but they are nude, with smiling faces, and are expressed with more freedom and individuality. The achievement of the Greeks in breaking through the barriers of dark superstition and fear into the enlightenment of clear thought is symbolized by these Archaic figures of gods, who seem to be walking out into the daylight toward us. The Greek gods were portrayed as men, in contrast to the animal-headed monster gods of earlier religions.

Many small Egyptian carvings must have found their way to Greece in its early days. The Phoenicians were the traders of those times, and their ships called at ports all round the Mediterranean. They also bought and sold works of art, including imitations they made themselves, so that traces of many styles are noticeable in early Greek art. But as it changed and developed, it became something peculiarly their own, reflecting the extraordinary originality of their outlook. They were intellectually adventurous, and were the first people to look for a rational explanation of the universe; their humanism led them to study man in all his aspects.

In comparison with the Egyptians, whose sculpture maintained a level course for more than two thousand years, the Greeks span of development is incredibly short—it rose and fell within a few hundred years. The Archaic sculpture of the sixth century changed to the Classical style of the Parthenon during the fifth century, when Pericles was ruling in Athens, and before the end of the fourth century, the decline had already begun. During this short time, the poets, playwrights, mathematicians and philosophers were producing those works which have stimulated the people of the world ever since, and whose effect is felt to this day. In them, can be found something of significance applicable to every age, and this accounts for the perpetual discovery and rediscovery of their genius in all its aspects.

The spreading of Greek thought, knowledge and art began immediately. The Greeks travelled widely—merchants, craftsmen sailors, and mercenary soldiers. During the third century B.C., when Greece became impoverished, many artists left the mainland and went to work for private patrons in Alexandria, Syracuse, and other Greek possessions. But their sculpture during this Hellenistic age deteriorated, and little remained of its former greatness. After the Roman conquest in 146 B.C., Greek artists were exiled or enslaved in Italy, copying the enormous number of Greek sculptures that had been carried off by the Romans.

THE ETRUSCANS

The Greeks' contemporaries in Italy, the Etruscans, were also a republic of aristocratic citizens, but very little is known about them or their origins. The materials they used were terracotta, bronze and some stone.

THE ROMANS: 200 B.C.–A.D. 400

The Romans had a particular talent for acquiring ideas, techniques and materials from other nations and adapting them for

their own purposes. Architecture was the art that came most
naturally to them and for sculpture they employed the Etruscans
as well as the Greeks. Marble and bronze were the materials
favored by the Romans, and there are no indications that wood
was ever used.

During the first and second centuries, A.D., the Roman Empire
was only equalled in power by China which was even greater in
area and population. These two Empires dominated the civilized
parts of East and West simultaneously, in almost complete
ignorance of each other, until about A.D. 200. Then, weakened
by a plague and by the continual attacks of barbarians, they both
began to decline and finally to disintegrate.

At the same time, Christianity gradually ceased to be an under-
ground movement, and soon after A.D. 300, was adopted as
Rome's official religion. The Emperor Constantine moved the
capital away to the safer and more peaceful Byzantium, but the
Pope stayed in Rome, and toward the end of the fourth century,
the two capitals became rivals for power. The Empire divided into
two, and while the Greek half withstood barbarian attacks and
all attempts at invasion for another thousand years, the Latin
half, together with Spain, France and England, were overrun by
robber-armies. These countries were divided into many small
separate territories, ruled over by barbarian chiefs.

THE DARK AGES AND EARLY CHRISTIAN ART
400–1000

During the fifth century, the cities of Europe stood empty and
impoverished; the Roman roads fell into ruin and the countryside
was neglected. The barbarian rulers kept up unceasing warfare
with each other and the only places safe and quiet enough to work
in were the monasteries.

Early Christian art had begun as Rome declined, the sculpture
consisting of reliefs on stone sarcophagi or ivory panels. The
sculptors were untrained, and when they attempted figures, they
copied the Roman sculptures of pagan gods to represent charac-

ters from the Bible and they also used many pagan emblems and symbols. But in Byzantium, the artists, being Greek, were far more skilled, and the renowned Byzantine style, which persisted unchanged right down to the seventeenth century in Greek and Russian icons, had its early beginnings in the fifth century A.D.

In A.D. 700, Byzantium forbade all image-making, whether in mosaic, painting or sculpture. This strict iconoclasm lasted for two hundred years, and many Greek artists left Byzantium to work for other monasteries in Europe.

The monastic workshops employed painters, ivory-carvers, goldsmiths, carpenters, metalworkers, masons and craftsmen of every kind, who provided all that was needed for the monastery chapels. This consisted of altar-furniture and candlesticks, caskets and book-covers, and reliquaries for containing the relics of saints. One of the best known of these reliquaries is at Conques in France: a crowned figure about two feet high seated on a throne and made of gold inlaid with precious stones. Many rich materials, precious metals and jewels were used at that time, but perhaps the most typical material of the age was ivory, of which they made panels, boxes and caskets, delicately carved with reliefs of Biblical and allegorical scenes and characters. They vary in style between Byzantine and Roman—the Byzantine figures being elongated and large-eyed, while the Roman figures look like senators: beardless, with short hair and wearing togas.

Wood carving seems also to have consisted of relief panels, such as those on the doors of Santa Sabina in Rome. Apart from these and the reliefs on stone sarcophagi and on stone capitals in the few Byzantine churches, sculpture was on a small scale.

An outstanding quality of all the relief-carving and craft-work was that it was all very similar in style whether it came from England or France, Ireland or Spain, Italy, Germany or Byzantium. The style was international, just as the Latin language was in those days, and it was circulated and perpetuated by monks, pilgrims and skilled workers, who travelled from monastery to monastery, despite the danger and difficulty. It was a mixed style;

a fusion of Classical and Byzantine motifs with patterns and rhythms of Eastern or Barbaric origin.

Arab design and decoration were included in it, but no sculptural influence, as the Moslems were forbidden, like the Jews, to make 'graven images'. The Moslem Empire, which stretched across the whole of the Southern Mediterranean including Egypt in the seventh century, affected the sculpture of other nations only indirectly. The Renaissance was partly due to the impact on Italian minds of the Arabs' learning and knowledge, their discoveries in science, mathematics and astronomy, and their rich decorative architecture.

ROMANESQUE PERIOD: 11TH AND 12TH CENTURIES

The Christian people had long been expecting that the end of the world was to come in the year 1000, and when this did not happen, a cloud lifted, and the sense of relief brought a wave of confidence and enthusiasm. This is one possible reason given for the sudden medieval renaissance of the eleventh century which was to continue for four hundred years.

The spontaneous use of large figure-carving on the many new churches may also be partly due to the lifting of the ban against images in Byzantium.

The term Romanesque comes from the type of architecture— round-arched like the Roman style. The churches are like fortresses, plain and compact with thick walls, and they are often situated high up on hills. The stone sculptural decoration was evidently planned with the building as a whole. That the masons carved the work *in situ*, is indicated by the fact that some of it was left unfinished.

Romanesque carving is full of feeling and zest. The figures are symbolic rather than drawn from life. They are often thin and elongated and seem to be floating or even dancing, in strange swirling draperies.

There is divided opinion as to how and where this Romanesque carving began. The most important source of their motifs was provided by the illuminated manuscripts in the monasteries, and the ivories, metalwork and textiles of the previous centuries. Nevertheless these flat drawings, and small ivory carvings only a few inches long, had to be enlarged tenfold, translated into stone and expertly rendered *in situ*. There was no carving tradition for the sculptors to follow, no system of practical training and experience. Yet they produced numbers of impressive figures in high relief, as well as intricate ornament, animals, birds and fabulous beasts.

The most likely examples for the carvers to base their work on would have been the Roman remains unearthed in Italy and the south of France—Roman capitals and columns, or fragments of sculptured relief and ornament.

In England, Romanesque style is known as Norman, and is even more massive and plain than the Continental. There are very few figure-carvings, and these are less accomplished than the French. It is interesting to notice that some of the Norman decoration is based on Norse and Danish wood carving. It is extremely flat and linear, so that in a photograph, it can easily be taken for wood rather than stone. In later centuries, the Scandinavian wood carvers in their turn were influenced by English stone carving.

Some wood carving from the Romanesque period is still left in the early European churches. It is to be found in reliefs on stall-work, doors and bosses and there are a few figures in the round which are almost always of the Crucifixion or the Madonna and Child. A very early head—originally from a Crucifixion—is at South Cerney, England. The Madonna figures are usually seated, with the child on their knees, and sometimes hold an apple in one hand (Fig. 57). They and the Crucifixions still show traces of painting and gilding. These figures are very simple but are carved with great feeling. They have wormholes and splits in them but being nearly a thousand years old, it is remarkable that they have survived at all.

Many works of art have been lost through the destruction of past civilizations, but the building of churches has helped to

Fig. 57. *Madonna and Child* in wood, approx. height 4 ft., German,
eleventh century, at Paderborn, Germany.

preserve them, by giving them permanent sites. Nevertheless,
while they have been treated with care because of their sacredness,
they have also been vulnerable to deliberate destruction. In
England, for example, the churches suffered on two occasions:
in the sixteenth century through the campaigns against popery,
and again in the seventeenth century, during the Civil War.

Besides this deliberate mutilation, sculpture has suffered through neglect at all periods, or has been replaced by later work. Craftsmen and architects were continually perfecting their work technically, and took it for granted that they were improving on what had gone before; aesthetic tastes changed, and until recent years work that we would have appreciated was constantly being destroyed.

THE GOTHIC PERIOD: 1180-1540

It is uncertain how the pointed Gothic arch first came to be used, but it had a revolutionary effect on architecture. It allowed the churches to dispense with thick walls and heavy columns, and to achieve more height, more space and bigger windows. This discovery led to an even greater outburst of building activity. In France alone between 1180 and 1280 five hundred churches and eighty cathedrals were built, and some of the cathedrals might have as many as five thousand figures, many over life size.

Building a cathedral must have been a tremendous undertaking at a time when manpower was the only force available. All the innumerable pieces of stone had to be moved and lifted, cut and fitted together by hand. It was a co-operative effort that included hundreds of masons, some of whom cut and jointed the stone, while others carved it. There were no 'architects' or 'designers' in the modern sense of the word, but there were master-planners who chose and fixed each theme or subject. The skilled mason—or 'imager' as he was called—then interpreted it in his own way, carving it directly into the stone.

When a great building was being constructed expert craftsmen came to it from all over the country, and when it was finished, moved on to another one. The 'lodges' where they stayed—the origins of the Masonic Lodges of today—were also used as tool houses and workshops. Later they became training centers and were usually established near the quarries. During the fourteenth century they became larger and more fully organized—being permanently staffed and able to supply sculpture in any form or size, to any part of the country. This meant that building and sculpture were no longer designed together, to the detriment of both.

It is obvious that from about 1200 onward the Gothic carvers had begun to study life. Designs were no longer adaptations of old manuscript drawings and ivory carvings, but were inventions based on the study of natural forms coupled with an intuitive understanding of what could most suitably be carved in stone. Like the Greeks of the fifth century B.C., the early Gothic artists observed nature with close understanding, and it was the rediscovery of Aristotle that inspired it.

During the fourteenth century, the church began to lose the confidence of the people, and the unanimity of thought and religion that had united the whole Christian world was falling apart. There was now less simplicity and austerity in the figure-sculpture and it became more realistic, more consciously graceful and charming. After the Black Death in 1350, the sculptors improved their technique still further and were extremely skilful in the realistic treatment of heads and hands, hair and drapery, but at the expense of coherent architectural design. Niches were left for the figures, which were supplied ready made. These late Gothic figures are full of invention and character study, but they have not the exquisite sculptural qualities of the thirteenth century when the advance toward a better technique went forward side by side with experiments in form and movement, treatment and design—each enhancing and stimulating the other.

Gothic stone figure carving was at its peak in the late twelfth and thirteenth centuries, stone ornament in the fourteenth century and wood carving in the fifteenth.

Gothic wood carving

Anyone entering a cathedral or church is so accustomed to the great amount of wood used in furnishing—pews, benches, choir-stalls, pulpits, organ-lofts, galleries and screens—that they might not think of examining it closely. But in an old church the woodwork is very unlikely to be all of the same period. At first glance, the old is often indistinguishable from the new, and the best work may be passed over unnoticed.

In the course of refurnishing the old churches in past centuries —'clearing out the old clutter', as one bishop expressed it—much of the woodwork used to be taken out and destroyed. In the nineteenth century, the old furnishings were often restored and 'improved', with new parts added and the joins camouflaged. But these Victorian Gothic Revival copies can be recognized by the fact that they are more mechanical in execution and lack the variation and slight irregularity of genuinely creative carving.

At the beginning of the Gothic period, church interior-work was in stone, and when wood was introduced, the carvers imitated the stone carving. The decorative tracery and pierced ornament were faithful and ingenious translations of stone originals and the few heads and figures still surviving from the early period have a solidity and shallowness of detail typical of stone but unnecessary in wood. Then, in about 1370, the wood carvers seemed suddenly to become conscious of their material and all its potentialities—to realize what freedom it would allow them and how much taller, lighter and more graceful their constructions could be. They became expert craftsmen and the fifteenth-century choir-stalls and screens, pulpits and font-covers show their technical brilliance and invention in the forests of tall pinnacles used as decoration. These continued to become more elaborate, both here and on the Continent, right up to the time of the Reformation. The stone carvers were meanwhile imitating the wood techniques.

English craftsmen were exceptionally skilled at wood construction of all kinds. The renowned hammer-beam roofs of the fifteenth century may be likened to the framework of an upturned boat and are built on the same principles. On these roofs, the beams and brackets are often terminated by figures of angels, kings or apostles—a double row of them all down the length of the nave—projecting at right angles to the wall and looking straight down into the church. As they are to be seen a long way off, these figures are very large and for the same reason are only roughly finished.

Judging from fragments that are left, most churches must have had a rood-screen: that is, a beam spanning the chancel with the crucifixion scene mounted on it—the cross in the middle and the figures of Mary and John on either side. These figures would certainly have been over life-size, and there must have been a great many other large wooden images, in niches and on altars,

Fig. 58. Carving of swan, choir-stalls, Lincoln Cathedral, England.

which have been destroyed. Wood is not so easily defaced as stone; the heads and hands of a wood carving cannot be struck off with a blow. But it is comparatively light and easy to remove and to carry away, and being dry and well-seasoned, must unfortunately have made good fuel for iconoclasts' bonfires.

Some wood carving, however, has been left undisturbed, and many small figures and animals can be found among the richly carved ornament on choir-stalls, bench-ends, poppy-heads and newel-posts (Figs. 58–60). Some of them must have been carved by the expert 'imagers' whose large works have been lost, but

C.M.

Fig. 59. *Poppy Head* at Eynesbury, England.

others have a naïve simplicity which suggests that they are the work of the ornament-carvers. It is as if figure-carving was regarded as a chance to put in something more personal—a change from the more disciplined repetitions of decorative work. The choice of subject and interpretation indicates great enjoyment and

J C.M.

Fig. 60. Carved panel on a bench at Altarnun, England.

amusement, particularly in the misericords, which are the most personally expressive of all the records left by the anonymous medieval craftsmen.

The misericords are to be found under the seats of the choir-stalls, which tip up on hinges. Each has a bracket or kind of shelf, which will give unseen support to anyone having to stand during a long service. The brackets are carved, always with a centerpiece and two 'ears', and the subjects are very often hum-orous, grotesque or satirical. There are scenes from pagan leg-ends and allegories as well as from the Bible, and there are also scenes of farcical episodes taken from their everyday lives. Some of these might be thought unsuitable for the decoration of a church, but Gothic art is full of surprising departures from the expected, and in any case, these misericords were normally out of sight in a humble position, so that the carvers were allowed to let their imaginations range wherever they pleased.

There are scolding wives and hen-pecked husbands; people with headache or toothache; people working: the miller, the sower, the reaper, the goldsmith, the boat-builder and the wood carver himself with a pet dog lying under his bench. There are men playing football, wrestling, hunting, hawking and taking part in tournaments, and there are numbers of fabulous beasts and birds and other fantastic creatures.

In the Biblical illustrations the characters are wearing medieval dress or armor; Noah's Ark looks like a three-turreted castle. Samson carries the gates of the city under his arm, like any medi-eval joiner delivering an order; Salome dances so vigorously that she even turns a back-somersault and in a boat-load of voyagers one is obviously feeling seasick.

The humor and candor of these very human and straight-forward comments on the way the carvers lived, add a great deal to the pleasure of looking at the carvings.

This kind of carving was polished, as paint would have rubbed off, but most statues were painted. In recent years, some of this painting has been renewed, and is sometimes disturbingly vivid. But it has to be remembered that in the Middle Ages, apart from life at Court, ordinary citizens saw very little color. They wore drab clothes of brown, black, dark blue and grey, and would enjoy the gilding and the brilliant colors in the churches. Stone figures used also to be painted, and the practice continued until the seventeenth century, when a fashion for pure white marble came in, and painting gradually died out.

Effigies

England is rich in effigies because they were spared when religious figures were destroyed, and there are a number of wooden ones still surviving. Only those that were covered with a plating of precious metal, like that of Henry V in Westminster Abbey, have suffered. The metal having been stolen, only the rough wooden core remains.

Wooden effigies were mostly made in the eastern counties, where stone was scarce, but they are to be found all over the country—often in small out-of-the-way churches. They portray knights, ladies and bishops, and in later years, from about 1360, rich merchants and their wives. Oak was the wood most commonly used and they were hollowed out from behind. This prevented them from splitting and the hole in the back does not show when they are in position on the tomb.

The early ones of about 1290 imitate the stone or Purbeck marble ones being made at the time and are flat, like reliefs of standing figures laid on their backs. Later the sculptors discovered how to make them look as if they were really lying down, and later still, for a time, the poses are given some movement. The knights lean on one elbow, have one knee raised or grasp their sword-hilts, showing how the sculptors had learned to take full advantage of their material. They are much plainer than the stone effigies, which have every detail of the armor incised and engraved on them. The wood effigies were gessoed to fill up the grain and make them smooth, and the detail was painted on. The paint and gilt having worn away, the carvings now appear very simple and bold in form, with qualities very similar to some sculpture of the present day (PLATE XXII).

The Continent is very rich in wood sculptures of the late Gothic period. They are carved with great skill, but in general, the technique is in advance of the conception and interpretation. Pulpits and canopies, screens and altars are fantastically elaborate and enriched with realistic sculpture, particularly in Flanders. Relief carving is so deep as to be like a stage-set. Scenes from the Bible are treated in a dramatic way, evidently derived from the medieval miracle plays. The backgrounds are like stage-scenery and the foreground figures are in such high relief as to be almost entirely in the round.

In Germany at the end of the fifteenth century, two sculptors were outstanding: Veit Stoss and Tilman Riemanschneider. Their wood figures vary in size from 5 or 6 inches to over life-size. Both have a recognizable style which stands out among the somewhat stereotyped works of their contemporaries. Heads and hands are taken from life but formalized, though not idealized. Indeed, many of their figures are character-studies of

Fig. 61. Wood drapery, sixteenth century.

plain, homely people. In common with all the wood carvers of the time, they were greatly interested in drapery. It is very complicated, often drawn forward into a bunch of great angular folds, carved very thin (Fig. 61). Again, it is studied from life but formalized, using to the maximum the resilient quality of the wood. Sometimes the German sculptors carved nude figures, which is rare in Gothic art, and is a sign that they were living at a time when ideas where changing. The beginning of the sixteenth century saw the end of the Middle Ages. The medieval way of living and thinking were dying out, together with their means of expression—Gothic art itself.

THE RENAISSANCE: 13TH–16TH CENTURIES

When England became Protestant, church-building stopped and many cathedrals and churches were left unfinished through lack of interest and money. It was a century before it began again, the first church being Inigo Jones's St. Paul's in Covent Garden. It has the first classical portico—with columns and pediment—ever built in Northern Europe. It is not only a gulf of a hundred years that separates this style from that of King's College Chapel in Cambridge which is Gothic. It is a revolution in taste, showing the effect of the Renaissance on England, although it had ended in Italy half a century before, and had already been superseded by the Baroque style.

Beginning in about 1260 with Nicola Pisano's sculpture, gradually rising to its zenith in the fifteenth century, and ending with Michelangelo's death in 1564, the Renaissance may be said to have lasted for three hundred years. It overlapped the Gothic period in other countries, but the Gothic style, being northern in origin, never really took root in Italy. It was Raphael who first used the name 'Gothic', to denote something outlandish and even barbaric.

The Italians were aware that they were living among the ruins of their own former greatness, and the classical style which had never quite died out, was a symbol of it. Everyone, rich and poor alike, was in sympathy with its revival. The architects used Roman forms as a basis and created an entirely new style, light and elegant. The sculptors went searching among the Roman ruins for fragments of sculpture, and their admiration for it is obvious in the way it influenced their own work. Unlike the sculptors of earlier periods who had also studied Roman remains, the

Fig. 62. Wings in wood and wing structure.

Renaissance sculptors were technically capable of equalling it and then surpassing it. At the same time, long-neglected Greek and Roman manuscripts were sought out and read avidly, and were later printed in book form. Philosophy and science could now be taken up again from where the Greeks had left them. The re-discovery of antique literature and of Greek writing in particular, caused a kind of ferment of quickened creative thought, in which intellectual advances and art kept pace with one another. By the fifteenth century, Italy resembled Greece of the fifth century B.C., in the extraordinary number of men of genius living and working there, and it is as difficult to account for the sudden upsurge of vitality and brilliance in one as in the other.

In the medieval world any urge to pursue a free and individual line of thought, or to search for rational explanations of human existence and natural phenomena were forbidden as heretical. The church supplied its own solutions to all problems and an answer to every question. But now, in Italy, these dogmas could no longer be blindly accepted. Even though the Pope himself lived in Italy, there was more free thinking and reasoning there than in any other country under his domination. This was partly because the universities were secular, not like those of the rest of Europe which had grown out of cathedral schools, and partly because Italy was receptive to new ideas and had always been in close contact with outside civilizations—the Greeks of Byzantium and the Moslems, from whom they gained knowledge of mathematics, chemistry and astronomy.

The church was still the chief patron of the arts but there were now many private patrons, wealthy citizens who were also scholars. They commissioned works of art and kept artists in their employ, giving them much more freedom to try out new ideas than church patronage would allow. The artists were stimulated by the new-found knowledge of anatomy, perspective, foreshortening and chiaroscuro, which gave them a wider comprehension of three-dimensional space, and so transformed their work that it lost all medieval naïvety.

Renaissance wood carving

Like the Greeks and the Romans, the Italians used marble and bronze, but there are still some wood carvings to be found among the hundreds of Renaissance works scattered all over the world, as well as those remaining in Italy (PLATE XIV). One of the most famous is the Mary Magdalene by Donatello in Florence. Less well known is his crucifixion, an early work which was originally painted in bright color, traces of which can still be seen under the brown varnish that now covers it. Its arms were fixed on in such a way that they can be turned round and altered from their horizontal position to hang down, in order that the figure can be placed in the tomb during Easter services.

Another of Donatello's wood carvings is a colossal wooden horse at Padua. It is very simple in form with a barrel-like body and its stance is similar to that of his bronze equestrian also in Padua, the Gattemelata.

Italian churches and cathedrals use more marble than wood for interior furnishing, but there are many stalls and benches enriched with carving to be found in them.

Influences of the Renaissance

The Italian Renaissance made a tremendous impression on the rest of Europe but was slow to make itself felt. Travelling and communication were still difficult between one country and another, so that few indications of what was happening had filtered through. When the French army marched through Italy in 1594, they were astonished and disconcerted by the strangeness of what they saw: the bold and spacious buildings, the round arches, garlands and cupids, so different from the Gothic architecture of their own country.

It was through books that Renaissance ideas first spread abroad. This impulse coming from Italy was a breath of life to the educated people of Europe and they responded to it by travelling to Italy and studying at the universities. They came back loaded with classical, scientific and medical knowledge.

The effect on England is seen in the spirit of discovery and experiment of the Elizabethan age, and above all, in the wealth of literature produced at that time.

Art in Europe generally was greatly affected; the expansion and enrichment of life and thought were increased by further inventions. Printed maps, ocean-going ships and the mariner's compass, all made it possible to explore overseas, and to bring back treasures and works of art, and all kinds of new materials. Chinese and Indian craftsmanship in particular caused great amazement and admiration.

Influences of the Reformation

Art was equally affected by the Reformation. The prestige of the church had fallen very low, and many of the rulers of northern Europe took the opportunity to break away from Rome. Europe became divided into two camps: Catholic in the south and Protestant in the north, with extremists on both sides.

In the Catholic half—Italy, Spain, Austria and South Germany —a movement known as the Counter-Reformation was started, which increased the wealth of the church once more, and hundreds of new churches and cathedrals were built. To impress the people, they were as ostentatious as possible, and contained as much decoration, ornament and sculpture as could be crowded into them.

There was a similar extravagant use of art and craft in France, but for a different reason. In this case it was for the glorification of the Monarchy. In England, and the northern Protestant countries, however, the arts had been brought almost to a standstill. Art and above all sculpture, were associated in people's minds with the luxury of court life, as well as with Catholicism and fears of idolatry.

THE BAROQUE PERIOD: 1600–1780

Although the force and the energy of the Renaissance had died away in Italy, it was there, after an interval of fifty years, that the new style known as Baroque originated, making Italy again a source of great influence.

After the death of Michelangelo in 1564, the artists who followed him had technical facility and assurance, but in imitating him they merely exaggerated his manner into mannerism. Lacking his power and intensity, their works were empty. It was the architects who led the way and evolved the *Baroque Style*.

In this age of growing technical virtuosity building-construction could be more complex and extravagant, daring and fantastic than ever before. Baroque architecture is plastic, like sculpture. Whole walls curve in and out as if giant hands had moulded them; there are broken pediments and flourishes and columns twisted like barley-sugar. But it is the interiors of the churches in Spain and Italy that are really overwhelming, with their gold and silver, sumptuous ornament, and multi-colored marbles. Not an inch of wall, floor or ceiling is left plain. Concealed lighting, false perspectives and optical illusions—all were used, as if by a theater-designer, to amaze the congregation.

The Baroque style was of great benefit to the Catholic Revivalists, as it drew the people back into the churches and overawed them with mystery and illusion. The sculptured figures emphasized movement—restless activity and dramatic energy. There were miracles and martyrdoms; saints in agony or ecstasy, with upturned eyes and agitated gestures. Sometimes real hair was used, real eyelashes and teeth, and pearls for tears.

Many of them were carved in wood, to make them light in weight and easier to carry in procession through the streets. Some of these figures are still used today, and may be seen in Easter processions, particularly in Spain. Even the newer ones will probably have been copied from the Baroque originals.

Each church has its own statue—Christ, Virgin, Pieta or Saint—and takes it to the cathedral to be blessed. It is mounted amid a forest of candles, on a wide platform carried by twenty perspiring men. They also have to carry a little boy or two, who scramble about on the platform, keeping the candles alight. The statue is borne along, up and down the hills, swaying and nodding, and the people in the streets clap their hands as they see it pass by. It has been repainted and in some cases dressed in real clothes, and is decked with precious stones, brought out for the occasion from safekeeping. Each one tries to be more glittering and more splendid than the others. Now and again, the procession stops, and is serenaded by Flamenco singers.

The attitude of the people toward their statues is now very much what it must have been when they were first carved. Baroque sculpture still lives in Spain at Easter.

The Italian sculptor Bernini (1598–1680) master of the Baroque in sculpture, dazzled his contemporaries. No technical difficulty stops him from posing his figures as freely as if they were real people caught in a moment of violent action. After the simple static movement of Renaissance figures, his are theatrical and sensational, and the crumpled drapery swirls out at the sides in undulating spirals or flattens itself on to the form, as if caught by the wind.

No one was able to carve marble as freely as he did, but some of his effects could be achieved in wood, with arms, legs, wings and drapery jointed on, and the joins all hidden by gesso and paint.

After Bernini, all sculpture had a greater freedom of movement, whether religious or secular, and stucco and wood painted and grained to imitate marble, were often used.

In France, the Baroque was more subdued because of a natural preference for the severely classical. The French kept to a more Renaissance style—they were the first Europeans to introduce it, and to welcome Italian artists. French landowners were buying art-collections of impoverished Italian noblemen— rather as America has been buying European art in the twentieth century—and building large country houses in imitation of Italian palaces. When Louis XIV built Versailles in 1660, it showed Baroque influence only in the extravagance of its enormous size. He kept thousands of courtiers there. Its interiors called for such quantities of ornament of every kind, and so many figures were needed for the façades, fountains and gardens, that a vast industry was organized and hundreds of craftsmen were trained to supply them.

During the following century, other monarchs and princes of Protestant countries tried to imitate Louis. They built their own versions of Versailles, and encouraged the arts and crafts of their country.

16th and 17th Century England

England also began to build many large country houses as well as churches but was even less sympathetic than France toward the extreme forms of Baroque.

The Renaissance style introduced by Inigo Jones had hardly been tried out in England when it was followed by Baroque. Both styles were explored simultaneously and Christopher Wren introduced certain Baroque elements into the exteriors of his fifty-three London City churches and of St. Paul's, while his interiors are more Renaissance in type, and are simple and restrained. They are light and open, with rich dark polished woodwork: reredos, pulpit, sounding-board, chancel-arch and screen, all of extreme elegance, and carved with high reliefs of wreaths, swags, flowers and fruit. Apart from small winged cherubs, there is no large-scale figure carving, no saints, Virgins or crucifixions. Puritanism remained strong and no 'images' were required. Even the cross as a symbol was not used again in England until about 1870.

Grinling Gibbons (1648–1720) is the most famous name in English ornament carving. In his own much narrower field, he was as daring and inventive as Bernini, and people marvelled at his work. His swags and drops of flowers, leaves and fruit (Fig. 18, p. 51) are carved to an extreme thinness, and he even carved a lace cravat for his own amusement. Like many of the master-craftsmen working in England at that time, he was of foreign origin. There were refugees from Catholic Flanders and Italians who had been brought over to introduce the Renaissance style of decoration. After the end of Gothic art, a new English tradition had to be started and new craftsmen trained.

English church interiors became more ornate, with colored marbles and a variety of materials; tombs and monuments were no longer in the form of recumbent effigies but were gradually becoming more elaborate. St. Mary Woolnoth, Nicholas Hawksmoor's City of London church (1716–1727), is typically English Baroque, with carved wood barley-sugar columns. Pure white marble was now the favored material, and figures were no longer painted.

A great deal of rich and splendid wood carving can be seen in the English country houses of the sixteenth and seventeenth centuries. There are carved chests, screens and coats of arms, lions and griffons, and magnificent staircases and chimney-pieces. There is a lively mixture of styles; as in the elegant linear Renaissance design carved on stout four-sided English balusters.

Rococo: 1720–1780

The eighteenth century is known as the Age of Reason, or the Age of Enlightenment. It was the age of the first encyclopaedias, museums, dictionaries, scientific treatises and historical researches. There was speculation about every aspect of life, and it can be recognized as the beginning of the modern age, not only in material advancement and scientific invention, but also in the more humane and liberal attitude to life.

At the same time, life at court and among the aristocracy became more extravagant and luxurious, particularly in France. Its artificiality was satirized by such writers as Voltaire and Rousseau, and among his many other advanced theories, Rousseau advocated a more natural life in natural surroundings. The sophisticated among his readers liked this novel idea of rural simplicity, and grand ladies dressed up as shepherdesses and milkmaids, though they were doubtless terrified of cows. This fashion is reflected in the sculpture.

The style of interior furnishings, ornament and sculpture became lighter and more frivolous, and the decoration more graceful and delicate. The heavier Baroque scrolls, swags and festoons were replaced by elegant linear designs in shallow relief, with shells, vase-shapes, ribbons and fans. The marble columns and pediments introduced into the interiors by Baroque architects, were now imitated in painted wood, stucco and plaster. The craftsmen of the Rococo period found out the possibilities of plaster as a material in itself—its lightness and fineness. Another advantage was its cheapness; monarchs and dukes were chronically short of money, though as fond of display as ever.

The Rococo style began in France, but was taken up with particular enthusiasm in Germany, and German wood carvings

of this time are the very essence of Rococo, both allegorical
figures and religious ones. All have a somewhat worldly look,
whether the subject is a saint, an 'Autumn', or an Apollo.

While Baroque angels and saints are in arrested movement
halfway out of their niches, Rococo figures have stepped out
altogether. These strange figures are generally of lime wood,
hollowed out, painted and gilded, and are masterly in execution.
No other material could serve so well as wood for outstretched
arms and hands with outspread fingers, for hair in corkscrew
ringlets, fluttering draperies and wings with thin, individually-

About 1775
Fig. 63. Rococo ornament.

carved feathers. Many of the figures are perched on the edges of
altars and cornices; some are fixed to wall or balcony and seem to
be floating free. All the special properties of wood are made use
of, where stucco would be too heavy and plaster too fragile.
In marble monuments of that period, small projecting parts are
sometimes found to be made of wood painted to look like marble
and added on afterward.

The chief characteristics of the Rococo style are restless movement and avoidance of all symmetry. An ornamental frame will
be designed and carved so that its center-line has been shifted
and curved to one side at the top (Fig. 63). It is carved very thin,
or into a spikiness which is a feature of the style.

In England, decorative motifs are Rococo in feeling, but the dislike of oversumptuous extravagance and exaggeration still prevails. Exteriors retain a classical simplicity, and interiors show that English craftsmen had an unerring taste and sense of proportion in everything they designed and made. The eighteenth century—the Georgian Period—is the apex of English architecture and furniture-making.

Interiors of churches and houses are remarkable for their exquisite plasterwork, which enhances the elegance and spaciousness of the architecture. Some wood carving is to be found, but plaster was quicker as well as cheaper, because moulds could be used for repetition work.

Wood was evidently considered unsuitable for statuary, which was of marble or bronze—to be in keeping with the Roman fragments and Renaissance works that were being imported in great numbers.

Anyone who goes to look at the wood carvings in the Victoria and Albert Museum in London, a wonderful collection—will not find many English examples. These are still in their original settings in cathedrals, churches and houses, and among them can be found many small reliefs, heads and monuments from all periods, anonymously carved by the local woodworker. In the Museum, the carvings are mostly German, Flemish or Spanish.

Sculpture in Europe generally had lost its foremost position among the Arts. After the Renaissance, when reading and research became more widespread, and the thoughts and ideas of the people more complex and many-sided, the other arts—painting, music, the theater and the novel—were found to be a more suitable and flexible means of expression than sculpture. Painting had developed side by side with sculpture in Italy; literature, drama and music had been encouraged and advanced at Versailles and all the smaller courts; and there were now as many secular patrons as religious ones. Artists' themes were non-religious as often as religious. Handel used some of the tunes originally intended for his operas, which had libretti based on pagan legends, in his religious oratorios.

NEO-CLASSICAL AND ROMANTIC PERIODS
1780–1880

Toward the end of the eighteenth century, there were fresh changes. The French Revolution undermined ideas which had always been taken for granted; everyone's attitude to life was shaken and the old system of values was questioned. The Industrial Revolution though less violent was equally disturbing. With the invention of the blast furnace and the steam-powered engine, man is said to have taken a step forward in controlling the forces and materials at his command, greater than any since the Stone Age. The immediate consequences, factory building and the mushroom growth of towns, which were beginning to disfigure the English countryside, were indications of the future that was in store.

The resulting response was the Romantic movement which swept like a wave over the whole of Europe, lasting nearly a hundred years. It had much wider implications than the Neo-Classical movement, which was purely an art-style. This style arose through a renewed enthusiasm for Classical art which made the sculptors turn against the Rococo style as frivolous. They now aimed to create a more noble and dignified kind of sculpture based on the Antique and exact measurements of ideal form. The Roman sculptor, Canova (1757–1822), was the leader of this movement and in his day he was considered to be 'greater than Michelangelo'. The aesthetic taste of his age may be indicated by the fact that the newly discovered fragments of genuine fifth-century Greek sculpture, including the Elgin Marbles, were not yet appreciated; they were thought to be clumsy and lacking in 'ideal beauty'. Roman copies and late Hellenistic work were preferred. The Neo-Classical style continued into the Romantic movement and became part of it; in the end it was largely a question of using correct Grecian costume and hair-styles.

A school of English-born sculptors at last appeared in England influenced by Canova and working in the Neo-Classical Romantic style. It was they who created the huge marble monuments in Westminster Abbey and St. Paul's.

The style of the Romantic movement is essentially literary in origin and English literature was the first expression of it. According to the dictionary a Romance is 'a tale of Medieval Chivalry, or a novel with that kind of subject'. Romantic is defined as 'strange, picturesque, imaginative, sentimental'. It implies a mood of antipathy toward the present and a desire to escape into the past—into some past age, that seems more to resemble the ideal world of the imagination, and the kind of life lived by the Greek hero, the Medieval Knight or the rustic shepherd.

Looking back nostalgically to medieval times was a prevalent mood in the early Romantic period, and for the first time in nearly three hundred years, Gothic art and architecture were admired once more. At first, this admiration showed itself simply as an attempt to evoke the Gothic atmosphere. Country houses were built in the form of sham castles and sham abbeys in the 'Gothick' style (although they often had severe classical interiors), and there were mossy dells, grottoes and 'wildernesses' in the gardens. Individual choice of architectural style became the vogue, in direct contrast to the practice of the previous century, the Georgian period, when all building was in harmony. It was a reaction against that period's great regard for order and reason. However, in casting off these disciplines they also rejected the good proportions of Georgian architecture and thus contributed to the muddled architectural ideas of the nineteenth century and the general deterioration of taste.

During the early phase of the Romantic movement there were two main styles in architecture: the Gothic and the Neo-Classical. The Houses of Parliament are a compromise; a classical shape with Gothic decoration superimposed. The man who designed the decoration, Pugin, was one of the pro-Goths who finally won this Battle of the Styles as it was called. After 1840 hardly a Classical building was put up for a generation.

To Pugin, Classical buildings were 'pagan gin-palaces', and he proved—so he said—that Gothic was the true Christian architecture. Pugin went to work for a very powerful society called the Ecclesiologists, formed to promote Gothic art, and the Gothic Revival began in earnest.

The picturesque Gothic of the earlier Romantics was considered flippant and their light-hearted sham ruins deplored. During this later phase of the Romantic movement, a sober Gothic style was used, not only for churches, but for town-halls, schools and railway stations. But correct Gothic ornament had not been used in England since the sixteenth century and no craftsmen able to carve it successfully could be found. Pugin published engravings of Gothic detail and set up workshops for teaching it.

Other workshops for craftsmen were afterward started by such men as William Morris, a vigorous pioneer of the Arts and Crafts movement which still exists in England and has been imitated by many other countries. The movement represents a protest against the harm done by the factory system, which divides the work into a series of small processes and destroys a man's interest. Although it is impossible to put the clock back, such spontaneous protests draw attention to what is happening, if only by pulling in the opposite direction.

The workshops and training-centers meant a revival of wood carving although it was only for ornament. In the places where wood carving had never died out, it was more of a peasant art, with traditions and methods handed down from father to son. Carved wooden crucifixes and saints for wayside shrines and village churches in Catholic countries, and all kinds of figures, animals and toys are still to be found in many of the thickly forested areas of Europe.

Another form of traditional carving—the big, hand-carved wooden figure-heads for sailing ships—can be seen in the splendid collection on board the Cutty Sark at Greenwich, England. They are boldly carved and full of character.

The academically trained sculptors of the nineteenth century still only used marble and bronze, and the marble carvings were executed less by the sculptor's own hand than ever before. The increasing facility in the use of the pointing-machine meant that the sculptor, after making a clay model, would send it away to be turned into marble by expert anonymous 'ghost' workers. The pointing-machine is a means of reproducing a plaster model in stone by drilling hundreds of holes to a correctly measured depth into the stone, and then carving away the surplus. It is a method unsuitable for wood.

Typical of the late Romantic period are the large, grandiose statues of statesmen, generals, admirals and bishops, that stand about our towns and cathedrals, or the sentimental, idealized female nudes which filled the Royal Academy year by year.

THE BEGINNING OF THE MODERN MOVEMENT

The first sculptor to react against them and their banality was Rodin. Like his contemporaries, the Impressionists, he accepted nature as he saw it, never deliberately idealizing or beautifying it, or glossing over the fact that it is very seldom 'perfect'. His work was thought to be ugly and therefore shocking. It remained controversial for years, like that of Maillol, another French sculptor born twenty years after him, and was not appreciated until the early years of this century. Maillol's simplification of form, based on early Greek sculpture, made his work impersonal, and it illustrated no subject—unlike the contemporary academic figures which were expected to illustrate a theme, personify a legend, or embody some edifying sentiment.

Maillol had been an assistant in Rodin's studio and three other sculptors who worked for Rodin in their youth also became famous afterwards: Despiau, Mestrovic and Bourdelle. All of them used a variety of materials, including wood; Rosandic, a fellow Yugoslavian of Mestrovic, worked almost entirely in wood.

The gulf between the official, academic art and the work of the individual artists of advanced ideas, was now widening, and from about 1870, when the first Impressionist exhibitions were received with sarcasm and ridicule, the two forms of art have to be differentiated.

The use of a great variety of materials was one of the most important aspects of the change that was taking place in sculpture. It was realized that marble was maltreated through the use of the pointing machine, being forced to imitate clay models without taking into account its own characteristic qualities. In the early decades of this century the younger generation of sculptors began direct hand carving in their studios, and wood finally came back as a sculptor's medium.

PRIMITIVE ART

This is perhaps a suitable place to speak of primitive art, as it is the time when it first began to make a strong and lasting impression in Europe.

The nineteenth century saw the first archaeological expeditions to many countries, beginning with Egypt. Napoleon, inspired perhaps by the uncovering of Pompeii in 1760, took scholars and artists with him when his army invaded Egypt in 1800, and the people of Europe were amazed at the drawings, records and works of art that were brought back. Egypt had remained silent and unknown for nearly a thousand years; a few descriptions in neglected Greek and Roman books; a few seemingly far-fetched travellers' tales were all that had been known of her former magnificence.

Excavations were next started in 1840, in Mesopotamia and then in Mexico; Mycenae in 1870 and Crete in 1890. Besides the works of art brought back from these ancient centers of civilization, other kinds of treasure were accumulating, taken from countries at earlier stages of civilization than our own. From the sixteenth century onward, primitive works of art and craft had been brought home by travellers, explorers and colonizers.

The craftwork—the pottery, weaving, fretwork carving and basketwork were popular and found their way into contemporary drawing-rooms, but the wood figure-carvings and masks were considered to be curiosities—heathen idols, unsuitable for a

Christian home, and many of those not put in museums must have been thrown away.

Some of these wood carvings certainly have a frightening appearance. Even behind glass in a museum case, prosaically lit by electric light, they give out their own atmosphere of weirdness and mystery. The fetish figures in particular, still with a forest of nails or knives sticking in them, suggest associations that are grisly in the extreme. How they must have looked in their original settings may be imagined—in the dark huts or temples, in the gloom of tropical forests. That is the kind of lighting they were designed for, each carving having been specially made for its intended position. The rough finish on some, and their sharp, contrasting planes, would be all the better for making a strong effect in such a light.

Seeing these figures in their dimly-lit settings, must have been an overwhelming experience for the first white conquerors; they and the missionaries who followed them are known to have destroyed a great many, in their zeal for converting the natives. Carving died out altogether in some places; in others, it increased again after a pause, to supply the modern tourist with souvenirs. In many cases, this is a question of copying the same pieces over and over again—expertly but mechanically—and the resulting works are not to be compared with the originals.

The impact of the primitive world on the white pioneers was strong, but was more than equalled by the effect of their arrival on the native populations. At first, they thought the white man was a character out of their own legendary past—some mysterious supernatural being, come back from the dead.

But after they had recovered from their fear, they began recording their impressions of him in painting and sculpture, the earliest being the bronze figures of Portuguese soldiers found at Benin, wearing sixteenth-century uniforms and carrying guns. The gun is observed with great accuracy whenever it appears in primitive portraits of the white man, being the source of his most potent magic, and other emblems are treated with great attention—articles which have aroused the natives' curiosity. He may be shown

wearing a top hat, smoking a pipe, carrying an umbrella; sometimes holding a bottle and glass. His buttons are made much of,
and so are his boots and his beard. African tribal chiefs still wear
a top hat and carry an umbrella as signs of power and privilege.

There are even some African wood carvings of European
women—schoolteachers, nuns and missionaries—with long skirts,
flat figures and rather plain, earnest faces.

Fig. 64. *Ancestral Figure*, Toromiro wood, Easter Island.

Other primitive carvings, done after the arrival of the white
man, such as the immensely tall totem-poles of British Columbia,
were carved with the aid of European tools.

It is in lands where the people live in forests and jungles, that
one would expect to find wood carvings, and this is generally true,
but there are exceptions. Many wood figurines have been and are

still carved on Easter Island, famous for its colossal figures in volcanic rock. At first sight, the island is treeless, and in fact, the only wood available is the Toromiro tree, which grows down beside the lake in one of the volcano craters. The shape of this wood has dictated the curved form of the statuettes made from it (Fig. 64). Even in the Arctic circle, where there are no trees at all, the people carve driftwood.

The places in which primitive wood carving has been most prolific includes ancient Peru, Polynesia, Melanesia, Indonesia, Alaska, Canada, and—the richest source of all—West Africa. Besides decorated objects of use and ornament, they produce figures in the round, animals, reliefs and masks. The training of the wood carvers seems to vary from place to place, but they evidently learned the technique at the same time as they were initiated into the proper magic rituals connected with image-making. The 'art schools' would be more like secret societies where the myths and legends of the tribe were handed on, together with the orthodox ceremonial rites. They were the equivalent of such Western institutions as University, Church, Library, Academies of Music and Dancing, and Art School, all combined into one.

West Africa

Each center had its own characteristics but the West African may be taken as typical. The so-called idols have their counterpart in the religious sculpture of Western civilizations; they do not portray deities to be worshipped. For the most part they represent devotees or—like Catholic saints—they are believed to have the power to intercede with the gods. An image of a woman holding a baby means a prayer for maternity. Many of the masks are for ritual dances, each with its special dance-rhythm and chant, and some are so big and heavy as to be tests of strength and endurance for the wearer.

An ancestor cult is common to many tribes. After someone dies, a figure is carved in which his spirit is supposed to dwell. These are the nearest things to portraits that are ever made. An actual portrait of a living person is considered dangerous, as he will suffer immediately any harm is done to the image.

Instead of a life-like representation of the human form, the carver's intention is to give a generalized version. He never uses a model directly, but always works from memory. The figures vary in size from a few inches to a few feet and are occasionally life-size or over. They may be standing, sitting, squatting or kneeling and the poses are static with no turn or twist of the body or head.

The figures are carved from one block of wood—either a piece of the whole trunk or a segment—and everything has to be fitted into its width. Even if the subject is a rider on horseback, the horse must be compressed and reduced until it is ridiculously small and insignificant. This does not trouble the African carver as he is accustomed to minimizing or even leaving out altogether anything unimportant, irrelevant or taboo, while increasing the size of everything worthy of emphasis.

There is a system of symbolical conventions laid down, as there was in Egypt, and no deviation is allowed. But Egyptian statues, being of stone, stood for centuries serving as models for succeeding generations. The African wood carvings had to be continually replaced and this made the traditional style much more flexible and susceptible to change. No one could call Egyptian sculpture naïve, and in the same way, African carving is far less naïve than it might seem. The carver uses symbols which are easily understood by the people, through which he can express innumerable shades of meaning.

These figures may look simple and straightforward but to copy one exactly would be far from easy. Many of the shapes come through the type of tool used, and from habitual muscular movements in handling it.

Each tribe has its own style, totally different even from its closest neighbor's. Some favor a rough-hewn type of carving while others put great emphasis on finish and rub palm-oil into the wood to polish it.

The skilled Negro carver knows all the many types of trees in his neighborhood and their special properties, so that he can select the most suitable for his purpose. Sometimes the choice is dictated by ritual but in general, the softer woods are used for masks and the hard woods for figures. His main concern is to find wood that will not split easily and that will be resistant to termites.

These observations are taken from present-day Africa where there are still a few full-time sculptors left, but it may be assumed that they also apply to the past. Some primitive communities are nowadays changing and disintegrating and the educated native begins to reject the tribal customs and beliefs of his ancestors, recognizing that they are rooted in superstition. But they are the source of his art.

It will be interesting to see what the African sculptor, with his great natural talent for carving, will produce in the future, after the inevitable introduction of modern techniques and tools, knowledge of anatomy and perspective, and Western standards of aesthetics.

African Carving and Modern Art

Modern Art—the subject of so much controversy—has grown and evolved from many different roots but its final development was certainly accelerated by the discovery of primitive art at the beginning of this century.

It is true that the more advanced of the artists were already receptive to these totally new and unexpected ways of seeing the human form. Its proportions had been altered and adapted to answer the needs of personal expression and design, in the works of the three outstanding Post-Impressionist painters of the older generation—Cézanne, Gaugin and Van Gogh. Cézanne's famous observation that nature could be represented by means of the cylinder, the sphere and the cone, seemed now to be given concrete proof by the African figures. Their geometrical forms, cylindrical legs and pear-shaped heads, reducing the figure to its simplest terms, were all that was finally needed to bring into being the new movement—Cubism.

It appears that two painters discovered a Negro carving in a Paris café-bar—brought there by a sailor. They persuaded the proprietor to part with it and showed it to Picasso. It so impressed him, that his next painting was partly based on it and contains the first signs of Cubist painting.

For people who take it for granted that 'likeness to nature' is the only criterion for a work of art, and that 'deal proportions' should always be given to the human figure, Cubism is at first incomprehensible. But in fact, neither naturalism nor idealization have ever been universally accepted. The Romanesque and Byzantine artists were unaware of such standards and the Baroque artists ignored them. The Baroque painter, El Greco, was unappreciated in the nineteenth century together with Byzantine mosaics, Romanesque carvings, Greek archaic figures and Italian Primitive paintings.

These works were passed over as crude and childish in the nineteenth century—unworthy to be called art. It is significant that they were all re-discovered at the same time as the Negro and other primitive carvings. They were completely outside the academic standards of the day, but perfectly in tune with the views of the artists already in revolt against those standards.

It is true that every great artist has revolted against accepted standards of form and has broken through them like a pioneer opening the way to future discoveries, but this had never been done so deliberately or so violently before.

Once the primitive works had aroused interest, there was no need to travel farther than a museum to look at them. They still had to be sought out, however, as they were being exhibited as curios, half-hidden among the paraphernalia of craftwork, utensils, weapons and other objects that had been brought back by indiscriminating travellers.

Museum curators have now arranged their ethnographical galleries so that the collections of primitive sculpture can be properly seen. Exhibitions are held in art galleries and are popular with the general public. Roger Fry wrote in 1920: 'One would like to know what Dr. Johnson would have said to anyone who had offered him a Negro idol for several hundred pounds. It would have seemed then sheer lunacy . . .' But Roger Fry himself might have been surprised that the unquestioned acceptance of African sculpture in our own time should be so complete.

Primitive works are unselfconscious and, being made by hand without attempting to disguise the fact, are an antidote to mass-produced machine objects. Having been made for a serious and definite purpose they are remote from any suggestion of exhibitionism to catch the eye of a possible buyer. These may be some of the reasons for their strong appeal. The African carvings are especially interesting to an artist because they are full of invention, with endless variations on the same theme, and they break all the anatomical rules with such conviction as to make it appear a matter of course. Perhaps their most remarkable quality is that they are essentially in the round. Each form is seen as a three-dimensional mass and there is no sign of the 'four-side approach' apparent in early Archaic Greek sculpture and often in the work of beginners. In these cases, each of the four sides is treated as a relief, whereas in a mature work, the contours can be seen to change, merge, free themselves and dissolve, as the spectator walks round it, like a landscape watched from a moving train.

Early in the twentieth century artists were trying to find a common denominator for all art—the indefinable factor which can bridge any gap of time, distance or national frontier. In attempting to isolate this quality, the artists left out of their works anything that seemed irrelevant, superficial or unimportant (unlike the academic artists of the time, who put in everything), thus bringing them down to the bare essentials: form, design, balance and rhythm. It was then a short step from non-realistic art to non-representational art—in other words, Abstract Art. If form and design are all that matter, then logically nothing else should be necessary, and all human associations may be eliminated.

The development of non-realistic and non-representational (also known as non-figurative) art has been the most important innovation in the modern movement, and both have given rise to a number of other movements and a great variety of different styles. Of these, Expressionism is the most notable. It may be defined as the expression of the artist's personal inner vision rather than of the world about him. It is therefore the opposite of Abstract Art, which, as we have seen, is an interpretation of the outside world. These two differing points of view, Expressionist on the one hand and Abstract on the other, are the modern equivalent of the divergence between Romantic and Classical art; that is whether the emphasis shall be on subject and emotion or on form and design. All are represented in every work of art but in varying degrees according to the temperament of the artist.

Henry Moore's approach is the Classical one; his abstract and semi-abstract compositions are based on life; not only the human figure, but on the infinite number of forms in nature which have particular significance for him (PLATE xvii). A study of living plants and trees, the formation of the landscape itself, and the small natural objects to be found in it—fossils, bones, flints, shells and pebbles—have given him an insight into the special qualities of wood and stone. His wood carvings, both large and small, have an elegance of treatment which proves his sensitive appreciation of every type of wood he uses. He always finishes his wood surfaces with a delicate polish which emphasizes the grain.

Epstein was a great sculptor of portraits modelled in clay for bronze, but he never carved wood. It suited his character better to pit himself against a more intractable material—the hardest stone he could find. His carvings were vigorously hewn out of large blocks, leaving the toolmarks still visible, and for them he took timeless, universal themes which he interpreted through the expression of his extremely powerful and personal inner vision. In treatment and style, these carvings may be regarded as Expressionist.

The freedom of the artist to give full rein to individual self-expression and individual choice of style and treatment, has never been greater. This has destroyed any coherence in development and has prevented that slow growth of a tradition which was normal in the past. The confusion of art-styles reflects the growing complexity of this century including its many new ideas, philosophies and changes in human thinking. Freud's discoveries in psychology and his emphasis on the sub-conscious part of the mind with its dreams and fantasies, have had a strong influence on art. One of its signs was the Surrealist movement of the thirties, which used the irrational incongruities of dreams as subject matter.

This aspect of life had previously been expressed in art, but this

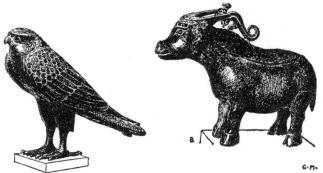

Fig. 65. Bronze animals. (a) Hawk, Egyptian, XXVIth dynasty (c. 650–30 B.C.). (b) Water buffalo, Chinese Chou dynasty (1122–256 B.C.).

was the first time it was used solely as the theme. The interest in child-art in this century is another indication of the preoccupation with psychological ideas, and a more recent sign is the belief that art can even take a step beyond the sub-conscious into the non-conscious regions of the mind. The exhibiting of monkeys' so-called painting was an extreme attempt to prove this. In Action painting, the advanced style typical of the fifties, the painter aims to shut off his conscious mind and in putting on the paint to make the action of his hand as undeliberate and fortuitous as possible, so that self-expression may come unawares.

Action painting has its equivalent in sculpture. Abstract shapes are constructed in welded metal or in any material that may be at hand: wire, wire-netting, small wood-blocks, steel rods or old scrap-iron, crushed and welded together, with the bits of machinery and machine-parts still recognizable. Many of these sculptures are robot-like and give a sinister impression. Their surface is mechanical, and the hand of the sculptor nowhere in evidence; the sculpture converges toward engineering and is equally impersonal. Paradoxically, the effort to reach the extreme point of personal inner consciousness has produced works which give a sense of complete anonymity, as they lack the individual 'handwriting' which normally distinguishes the work of one artist from another.

This art-form is known as Abstract-Expressionism, which might seem a contradiction in terms. But both types of artist work within it, each borrowing from the other. The Expressionists use abstract forms in their own way, just as the Romantic artists took over the themes, poses and costumes of Classical art. They give their works evocative titles, expecting the spectator to draw on his own imagination and read into them his own meaning and interpretation. But in its true sense, Abstract Art should, like music, be free of associations, and should not raise such questions as: what is its meaning, or what is its purpose, which are obstructions to an open mind. The intention is to be accepted, as architecture and ceramics are accepted, where the function is obvious and the abstract quality inherent.

Abstract Expressionism has been widely adopted in America, and it seems to stress an intense reaction toward intricate modern machinery and steel construction work, which may be one of attraction or repulsion. It is essentially a city-dweller's form of art.

Sculpture and painting are not the only arts experimenting in this way. Electronic music is composed by means of a series of purely mechanical sounds recorded on tape; plays are being performed with disjointed dialogue and no plot, for which the audience must find their own meaning and interpretation.

Forms of art change as they have always had to change. If

they were used for too long, they became worn out and only resulted in pale and feeble imitations of the great men who originated them. They needed to be revitalized and invigorated, and by drawing on some untapped source of the past, some of the necessary stimulus had been supplied.

Today, these potential sources are continually multiplying; the choice is so great that new styles follow one another with ever increasing rapidity. Galleries and museums exhibit art from every place and period; books of reproductions are published and widely circulated in all parts of the world. This gives the artist the unprecedented experience of being able to apprehend the whole range of art without even leaving his own country. Every nation may now share the entire world-tradition and this has contributed to the fact that an international style is now

Fig. 66. Stone carving on Notre Dame, Paris.

appearing again, as it did in the Dark Ages. A new work can be photographed and publicized within a few weeks, through the distribution of periodicals from one end of the world to the other.

The tendency for ever increasing speed is apparent in every side of life. Many sculptors prefer to use materials that can be quickly handled and will give quick results. Wood carving is comparatively slow. But the amount of lasting satisfaction a work of art can give, is governed to a great extent by the amount of thought, consideration and feeling that has been put into it, and in this sense, the slowness of wood carving may be a great advantage. The gradual development of a carving may give the modern wood carver a sense of connection with the past, a bond with the early carvers, whether in Europe of the Middle Ages, or Egypt of four thousand years ago.

Appendix A

I HAVE included the following by Mr John Linfield, the young painter, as I feel that it is of particular interest to anyone attempting a wood carving for the first time. It is a personal account of his own experience.

THE WOLF'S HEAD

A First Wood Carving, by John Linfield A.R.C.A.

Toward the end of a recent art school term in mid-summer I had just completed the Intermediate Examination in Arts and Crafts. During the course I had made a number of carvings in Maltese stone, Bath stone and the beautiful fossil-marked Hoptonwood stone. One day I was asked to make a wolf's head totem pole for the local wolf cub pack. The result of this request is illustrated in PLATE XXIV.

Although the art school I attended did not specialize in wood carving, I was anxious to undertake this commission and to get experience of a new material. A search in the art school garden discovered a tree trunk section of elm. The wood had obviously been felled some years before and appeared to be well seasoned. Elm wood was a good choice for this job owing to its resistance to the weather. A totem pole, after all, would often be carried in procession on rainy days. There was little time before the end of term, except to get a little advice and to borrow a few tools. I then took the block home to my improvised studio, the garden shed (Fig. 67).

The piece of elm measured about 12 in. high and the diameter of the tree trunk was approximately 18 in. First I selected the best part of the wood for the main carving of the head, avoiding a few slight 'shake' fissures. The plan, front and side elevations were then marked out in black poster paint. After preliminary saw cuts were made the spare pieces were put aside for the ears and base of the neck. I had borrowed one $\frac{1}{2}$ in. straight chisel,

157

Fig. 67. Carving the Wolf's head: drawing by John Linfield.

two or three gouges, ranging from ⅜ in. to ¾ in. and also one bent
gouge. In addition to these, there were also three 'G' cramps.
I made myself a mallet from a block of oak with an ash dowel
for the handle. I screwed a piece of 1 in. plank to the base of the
block of elm before cramping it to the bench.

I started the carving with the ¾ in. gouge and found that elm
wood was delightful to cut. I enjoyed the satisfying process of
carving, the curling chips, and the polished concave facets left
by the gouge. It was not long before I had roughed out a fairly
convincing wolf-head shape. By proceeding with a smaller gouge,
the carving gradually progressed. I made some research into the
character of the animal's head and also looked at early carvings
of animals such as the Iberian bronze deer of the eighth century
B.C., now in the British Museum. This gave me added inspiration.

I had now reached the stage when the carving of the mouth
had to be started. At all stages the shape was drawn again with

poster paint. Now I drew the shape of the tongue and teeth on the side of the head. I used the gouge with the bent shaft to remove the wood from the interior of the mouth. I then cut the tongue and teeth with the aid of both bent and straight gouges. All that remained now was to carve the ears and the base of the neck from the wood which had been set aside for the purpose. For the sake of strength, I arranged that the grain should run through the ear from root to tip. Two square-shaped recesses were then cut in the head and the ears carved at the base to fit. I then drilled a $\frac{1}{4}$ in. hole in each recess and fitted a $\frac{1}{4}$ in. dowel into the base of each ear. Then Scotch glue was applied liberally and I tapped the ears home. Considerable care was needed during the whole of this latter operation in order that the ears would appear in complete unity with the head. The joints, as you can see in the photograph, were not perfect, but they were extremely strong, and the small space on the surface was packed with woodfiller.

I roughly shaped the base of the neck and glued and dowelled it in position. When the joint was set I completed the neck shape.

The carved collar was enriched with boxwood studs. I felt that this would give greater interest to the lower part of the work. Each stud was first cut and then sandpapered to a high finish. Rasps and sandpaper were used to take away the tooled finish on the carving. I felt that the severity of a smooth surface would add to the visual impact of ferocity, characteristic of the wolf.

Final details included staining the tongue with red ink and waxing the whole head with a household colorless wax polish. Owing to the brown color of the wood the ink produced a dull red, not too violent to break the unity of the whole.

Thus the wolf's head was completed and I had proved that a piece of sculpture may be created by using very simple equipment, technically close to that used by the earliest carvers in wood.

Appendix B

Dish Carved in Brown Oak

(25½ in. × 12¾ in. × 1½ in.)

by David Pye

Brown oak tends to be brittle and is not a good carving wood. For work of this character it is possible to use it, but the sharp arrises between the flutes are apt to crumble in places even if the tool is ground very thin as if for cutting soft wood. Such a tool must of course be used with care on a wood as hard as oak, or pieces of the edge will break away, and only the finishing cuts should be made with it.

The quickest way to hollow such a dish as this is to use a curved adze ('Spout adze') like a very large gouge used somewhat after the manner of a hoe. This is followed by curved spokeshaves worked across the grain, and the bottom is then trued up with gouge cuts as seen in Plate xv.

Neither the spout adze nor the curved spokeshave can be bought nowadays: but large ordinary carving tools will accomplish everything they can do, though taking more time to do it. The important thing while hollowing (or while removing a large amount of waste wood in any circumstances) is that the job *shall be firmly held* on the bench or block. When the adze or axe hits the wood, or when the mallet hits the handle of the gouge, there should be a thud, not a bang. If there is a thud the tool is biting; if a bang, it is jumping back.

The inside of a dish should usually (with rare exceptions) be completely finished before the outside is touched. (Fig. 68). Once the outside is shaped the job is far more difficult to hold firmly. It might even have to be temporarily glued to another piece of wood to fit it: a great waste of time.

When finishing the outside, the dish may be held edgeways in a vise with a sandbag or a block of compressed cork inside it so that the rim is not touched by the vise, which bears on the sandbag instead. The waste wood can then be removed with a draw-shave or draw-knife. With a deeper dish the waste would be removed by chopping with a broad-axe on a chopping block or by sawing—which is often quicker because of the difficulty of supporting the dish while chipping. The outside is finished with

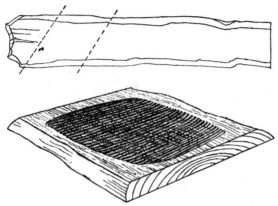

Fig. 68. Carving the Dish. (a) Diagram showing the section of wood used (as indicated by dotted lines), and (b) inside of the dish finished in the plank.

spokeshaves. Of these the kind with a wooden stock are incomparably better for carving than the cast iron ones. It is advisable to make the stocks oneself and to have several shaves of slightly different shapes. A spokeshave can be a most delicate and responsive tool and any wood carver doing large work can use it with great pleasure and effect. It must of course like all tools be properly sharp.

Index

162